Student-Powered
Podcasting

Teaching for
21st-Century
Literacy

Christopher Shamburg

International Society for Technology in Education
EUGENE, OREGON • WASHINGTON, DC

Student-Powered Podcasting
Teaching for 21st-Century Literacy

Christopher Shamburg

© 2009 International Society for Technology in Education

World rights reserved. No part of this book may be reproduced or transmitted in any form or by any means—electronic, mechanical, photocopying, recording, or by any information storage or retrieval system—without prior written permission from the publisher. Contact Permissions Editor at www.iste.org/permissions/; e-mail: permissions@iste.org; fax: 1.541.302.3780.

Director of Book Publishing: *Courtney Burkholder*
Acquisitions Editor: *Jeff V. Bolkan*
Production Editors: *Lynda Gansel, Lanier Brandau*
Production Coordinator: *Rachel Bannister*
Graphic Designer: *Signe Landin*
Copy Editor: *Kristin Landon*
Cover and Book Design: *Kim McGovern*
Proofreader: *Mary Snyder*

Library of Congress Cataloging-in-Publication Data

Shamburg, Christopher.
   Student-powered podcasting : teaching for 21st-century literacy /
   Christopher Shamburg. — 1st ed.
     p. cm.
   Includes bibliographical references.
   ISBN 978-1-56484-261-9 (pbk.)
   1. Internet in education. 2. Podcasting.   I. International Society for
   Technology in Education. II. Title.
   LB1044.87.S514 2009
   371.33'467876—dc22

                                  2009023669

First Edition
ISBN: 978-1-56484-261-9

Printed in the United States of America

International Society for Technology in Education (ISTE)
Washington, DC, Office:
   1710 Rhode Island Ave. NW, Suite 900, Washington, DC 20036-3132
Eugene, Oregon, Office:
   180 West 8th Ave., Suite 300, Eugene, OR 97401-2916
Order Desk: 1.800.336.5191; Order Fax: 1.541.302.3778
Customer Service: orders@iste.org
Book Publishing: books@iste.org
Book Sales and Marketing: booksmarketing@iste.org
Web: www.iste.org

Cover photos: left image © Corbis; center image © iStockphoto.com/Vladimir Mucibabic; right image © Corbis.

About ISTE

The International Society for Technology in Education (ISTE) is the trusted source for professional development, knowledge generation, advocacy, and leadership for innovation. A nonprofit membership association, ISTE provides leadership and service to improve teaching, learning, and school leadership by advancing the effective use of technology in PK–12 and teacher education.

Home of the National Educational Technology Standards (NETS), the Center for Applied Research in Educational Technology (CARET), and ISTE's annual conference and exposition (formerly known as the National Educational Computing Conference, or NECC), ISTE represents more than 100,000 professionals worldwide. We support our members with information, networking opportunities, and guidance as they face the challenge of transforming education. To find out more about these and other ISTE initiatives, visit our website at **www.iste.org**.

As part of our mission, ISTE Book Publishing works with experienced educators to develop and produce practical resources for classroom teachers, teacher educators, and technology leaders. Every manuscript we select for publication is carefully peer-reviewed and professionally edited. We value your feedback on this book and other ISTE products. E-mail us at **books@iste.org**.

About the Author

Christopher Shamburg is an associate professor in the Graduate Program in Educational Technology at New Jersey City University. Before teaching college he was a high school English teacher at the Hudson County School of Technology in Jersey City for 10 years and won several awards for his teaching, including Teacher of the Year, the Geraldine R. Dodge Award for Teaching Humanities, the Governor's Award for Outstanding Teaching, and two fellowships from the National Endowment for the Humanities. He has published and presented numerous articles and papers on educational technology. He is the author of *English Language Arts Units for Grades 9–12* (ISTE, 2008), and coauthor of *Teachers as Technology Leaders* (ISTE, 2006).

Chris is also a national workshop leader for the Folger Shakespeare Library's Shakespeare Set Free program and an English teacher for NJeSchool, New Jersey's largest online public high school, where he has developed English courses on podcasting and fanfiction. Chris is a founding member of Radical Teachers, a curriculum development and educational consulting company. He is a highly sought-after speaker and workshop leader.

Chris has his BA and MA from Rutgers in English literature and his doctorate in educational technology from Teachers College, Columbia University. He lives in Maplewood, New Jersey, with his wife Kate, and two children, Luke and Emma. Feel free to contact him at cshamburg@gmail.com or visit www.chrisshamburg.com.

Contributors

Lisa Bucciarelli is a foreign language instructor at Hinsdale Central High School in Chicago, Illinois. Lisa has her MA in Spanish and her EdD in Curricular Studies. She is a Google Certified Teacher and a Johns Hopkins University Adjunct Faculty member. Lisa has presented at numerous conferences and published articles within the realm of digital education.

Jeff Humphrey is a full-time instructor and administrator for the Digital Media Arts (DMX) Program at Touro College in New York City. He is completing his MA in Educational Technology from New Jersey City University where he earned his BA in Media Arts. He specializes in digital audio production and music technology. He is currently designing a professional development workshop focused on podcast production and its educational applications. Jeff is an accomplished musician and songwriter and performs regularly with his band in the New York area.

Kathleen Jerome has a Masters degree in Educational Technology from New Jersey City University and a Web Design Certification from Fairleigh Dickenson University. For her thesis, she ran a podcasting club for fifth- and sixth-grade students. She has taught engineering and technology to middle school students, from building paper furniture to creating databases of movie reviews. In her classes, she specializes in activities that keep the students engaged as they learn. Before pursuing her teaching career, Kathleen was a computer professional on Wall Street for many years.

Kate Mazzetti has her BA in English from Loyola College and her MA in Shakespeare Studies from the Shakespeare Institute in Stratford upon Avon, England, and she is an alumna of the American Academy of Dramatic Arts. She was an English and Drama Teacher for the Academy of Saint Aloysius in Jersey City, New Jersey, where she earned several teaching awards including the Geraldine R. Dodge Fellowship Award for New Teachers and the Douglass College Outstanding Teacher Award. She is currently a faculty member for Axia College, University of Phoenix.

Contents

Contents

Appendixes

Introduction

The podcasting projects in this book connect real-world applications, student interest, and powerful ideas for a variety of grades and subjects. We begin with the Foundations section, which focuses on the theoretical and technical issues of student podcasting and includes two tutorials on audio editing. The second section consists of seventeen stand-alone units, including several different audio dramas, a student-created media review, an audio tour, and a classroom journalism project. Each of the units includes an overview, procedures for implementation, a link to an example, and an assessment rubric correlated to a variety of national standards.

These podcasting projects are intended to be flexible models—to be tried, revised, modified, and extended based on your students, subject, and resources. The projects can be done in interdisciplinary teaching or in collaboration with a school library media specialist.

The projects in this book are correlated to seven sets of national standards:

- International Society for Technology in Education (ISTE)
  National Educational Technology Standards for Students (2007)

- International Reading Association and National Council of Teachers of English (IRA/NCTE) *Standards for the English Language Arts* (1996)

- American Association of School Librarians (AASL)
  Standards for the 21st-Century Learner (2007)

- World-Class Instructional Design and Assessment (WIDA) Consortium
  English Language Proficiency (ELP) Standards Grades 6–12 (2007)

- Teachers of English to Speakers of Other Languages (TESOL)
  ESL Standards for PK–12 Students (Grades 4–8 and 9–12) (n.d.)

- National Council for the Social Studies (NCSS)
  NCSS Curriculum Standards for Social Studies Update-Draft (2008)

- American Council on the Teaching of Foreign Language (ACTFL)
  National Standards for Foreign Language Education (1996)

Section I
Foundations

In these chapters I will first explain why you should consider podcasting with your students. We'll discuss how podcasting fits in with my ideas about 21st-century literacy, and how podcasting can be the catalyst for teaching powerful ideas that will stay with students for a lifetime. In Chapter 2 we'll take a close look at what podcasting is, and why it's different from simply placing an audio file on the Internet. Finally, in Chapter 3 you and your students will be able to dive in and learn how to use multitrack audio editing software by following a tutorial. This skill will provide the basis for all of the podcasting units in Section II of the book.

Chapter 1

Beyond Podcasting:
A Paradigm Shift

This chapter presents the big ideas of student-powered podcasting: how it can connect to ideas of 21st-century literacy, challenge existing educational paradigms, and become a catalyst for teaching powerful ideas.

Podcasting is the creation and serial distribution of media through the Internet. Audio and video files (often thought of as "episodes") are created and disseminated on a regular basis by a podcaster; a subscriber can easily receive new episodes and episode information, and download, view, listen, and transfer the episodes to a variety of portable players. Technical information on how to do these things is clearly presented in this book, but the true subject of this book is what students can potentially *learn* using this technology.

The specific technologies of podcasting offer an accessible and powerful tool that can engage students and give them skills for success in the 21st century. But the benefits of podcasting can go beyond technological proficiency and academic content knowledge, beyond enhancing the existing curriculum, and even beyond podcasting itself. Let me explain.

Podcasting offers an inexpensive way to create and share compelling media that correlates to authentic activities outside of school. Students who podcast become active participants in culture and society. They can create original content as they ethically and effectively collect and remix the work of others. Students can create audio dramas, news shows, or audio tours. This book gives directions, assessments, insights, and examples for a variety of multidisciplinary projects.

The ideas in this book began in 2006 when I was working with the NJeSchool, the largest online public high school in New Jersey. We were thinking about courses that would work **better** online than in a classroom, as well as broader questions about the types of projects, skills, and mindsets that students needed and the types of activities that they would like to engage in. After research, reflection, and some risk taking, we came up with a language arts class based on student podcasting that has been running ever since. Ultimately, however, we also came to realize that we had struck on a paradigm shift in curriculum development and teaching that correlated to larger social and technological trends and went well beyond the specific technologies of podcasting.

One reason the ideas in this book are a shift is because, as opposed to working from antecedents in education, the content was primarily developed from authentic activities outside of schools. The units in this book do not approach podcasting as an enhancement of the existing curriculum, but rather as a catalyst for reflection and curricular reform. Furthermore, though the technology is critical to the student projects, the ideas here are not simply about technological proficiency. The technology is a seamless part of real-world activities with educational value that connect to several disciplines.

Reading, Writing, Literacy, and 21st-Century Literacy

Although in this book I do address existing content standards and conventional literacies—reading, writing, speaking—my main premise is that students need to be directed in new literacies as well as conventional literacies. These new literacies cannot be simply tagged onto existing curriculum, models, and mindsets.

A shorthand way to describe literacy involves "reading and writing text," but the term literacy connotes a far more complex process. There have been distinctions between everyday literacy and academic literacy, for example, and an association of literacy with "discourses," or ways of acting in the world (Gee, 2004). In New Literacies, Lankshear and Knobel (2003) make an important distinction between the terms reading and literacy. They posit that the term reading conveys an internal, psychological process, while the term literacy conveys a social process—connected to other practices, communities, economies, and empowerment.

There has been a shift in education over the past 30 years to focus on literacy as opposed to reading—the changes are reflected in approaches, practices, funding, and program names. Two of the major factors that contributed to this shift from reading to literacy were, first, an awareness of the correlation between illiteracy and unemployment in the United States during the 1970s and, second, the growing trends in psychology and other social sciences to see learning as a larger social process as opposed to an isolated cognitive process (Lankshear & Knobel, 2003). This book looks at literacy both as the skills of reading and writing text and as the broader, complex social processes.

Moreover, it's the extension and clarification of these broader social processes that is the launching point of 21st-century literacy, the main focus of this book. It would be easy to dismiss the term 21st-century literacy as just another adaptation of the word literacy—at best, a term capturing a specific educational agenda, and at worst more jargon in the data smog. For me, the fundamental question "Why do we teach children to read?" helps clarify the importance of emphasizing what's unique about 21st-century literacy. We teach reading to enable participation and empowerment—we want students to succeed in the world, so it's important that they be able to understand others and communicate their own ideas.

Even a skeptic would likely acknowledge that for these goals to be realized in the 21st century, new skills and mindsets are required. Although specific technologies such as Second Life, microblogging, iPods, and podcasting could be included in the catalog of 21st-century literacy tools, the term *21st-century literacy* captures a skill set and frame of mind bigger and less ephemeral than proficiency with the latest technologies.

I believe that we are at a revolutionary point in our history, a paradigm shift akin to the introduction of writing to the ancient Greeks or the effects of the printing press on Early Modern Europeans. We need to look at our teaching in this larger sweep of history. Twenty-first-century literacies involve the skills and mindsets associated with the digital technologies and global networking of the information age. These skills and mindsets are related to the immediate technologies, but they are also related to the larger and tacit shifts associated with digital technologies and global networking—shifts in social structures, culture, capital, and labor.

There are some fascinating examinations of 21st-century literacy that informed the direction of my work with student podcasting and the ideas of this book. Prominent among them were Lankshear and Knobel's *New Literacies* (2003), William Kist's *New Literacies in Action* (2004), and Henry Jenkins' *Convergence Culture* (2006b), *Confronting the Challenges of Participatory Culture: Media Education in the 21st Century* (2006a), and the American Association of School Librarians' *Standards for the 21st-Century Learner* (2007). Below are common key ideas that informed the direction of this work.

> **Participation.** Digital technologies have given us unprecedented abilities to create media and content to express ourselves to various and wide audiences. Media creation tools and distribution networks that 20 years ago were available only to a handful of media conglomerates now come preloaded on even the least expensive computers. Almost anyone can create and distribute media and actively participate in culture, politics, and communities. Students need to identify appropriate venues for diverse media and content. They need the skills to compellingly create content for real purposes and real audiences. Our students need to be active creators, not passive consumers. They need to be engaged citizens and self-directed workers.

> **Appropriation.** Remixes, embedding media, and copying and pasting are part of the constitution of our digital environment. Students need the skills and mindsets to effectively and ethically synthesize the work of

others into original and compelling work. These skills are the foundation of audio remixes *as well as* good research papers.

Mediums. Students need to know that different mediums (audio, video, text) and different technologies (podcasting, online video, blogging) have different properties, purposes, advantages, and weaknesses. They need to learn how to identify, choose, innovate, and capitalize on these mediums and technologies.

Ethical Behavior. Students need to understand that with the opportunities possible with networked and digital technologies, there are also risks and responsibilities. We cannot teach this to students by blocking out the changing world, but must instead develop techniques to guide them in developing their own ethical compasses and responsible behaviors. They need to be able to identify ethical boundaries and existing abuses of new media.

Personal Interests. In traditional schools, students are often required to repress their individual interests and learn the curriculum of the school. Schools need to take a more dialectic approach between the goals of the school and the experiences and goals of the students. This not only correlates with much of the past three decades of research on cognitive science, but also matches the skills needed for today's world. As already mentioned, today's social and economic systems require more individual volition and portable skill sets. The ability to identify, hone, and connect personal interests to communities and organizations that value those skills is the path to a fulfilling life.

These are some of the premium skills for engagement and success in the 21st century, and podcasting is a powerful and accessible activity for teaching them.

Tensions and Conflicts

The skills and mindsets associated with new literacies are challenging many traditional paradigms of our culture. I believe they're also causing a need for a conceptual shift in our approach to education. It's worth highlighting some of the subtle but powerful paradigms that have outlived their usefulness in our digital and global world.

An increasingly blurry separation in society is the one between consumers and creators of media. Most of our systems—schools, law, entertainment—have been built on a strict separation between consumers and creators of content. Some of these systems—the United States legal system, for example—have built hundreds of years of precedents on this dichotomy. The recent explosion of digital technology that enables people to copy, share, and remix is a precipitous challenge to the workings of these systems. It's now more important than ever to educate students on the ethics and legalities associated with copyright, fair use, and the ethical appropriation of others' content.

In education, we generally strongly distinguish between individual and collaborative endeavors. But this dichotomy between independence and collaboration is not as simple outside of schools as we make it within schools. Our networked digital world facilitates and often even requires interdependence in both work and social life. I find that, using technology, many of my students spend their free time collaborating with, and receiving instantaneous feedback from, their peers—and they're tremendously engaged by it. The activities in this book attempt to harness that engagement.

In literacy and humanities education I see an unnecessary split between material that students are interested in and more traditional literature and curricular content. I would argue that students' perceived lack of interest in history, Shakespeare, poetry, or Jane Austen novels has nothing to do with history, Shakespeare, poets, or Austen, but with a teaching tradition that relies on rote memorization of facts, formalist essay topics, and the mechanics of literary analysis. If teachers would instead deeply reflect on what brings people to this material, students would more easily develop a natural affection for it. I hope the projects in this book will offer you new ways of approaching the material you teach that will truly spark your students' interest.

Cultivating Powerful Ideas

The units in this book are based on the space where real-world activities connect to student interests and powerful ideas. For this book, I define "real-world activities" as activities that occur outside of school and that are done in communities by professionals. Podcasting tours, news stories, audio dramas, and media reviews are examples of real-world activities. These activities come with their own goals, communities, examples, and models. The objective of the podcasting course was to find and refine activities that maximized student interest and choice. For example, in the audio tours lesson, not only do students choose a place of interest, but they focus on making the tours engaging and interesting to audiences of their choice.

Applying the term "powerful ideas" to educational technology was pioneered by Seymour Papert in his groundbreaking book *Mindstorms: Children, Computers, and Powerful Ideas* (1980). Papert saw technology as a catalyst for powerful ideas. He writes that "one comes to appreciate how certain ideas can be used as tools to think with over a lifetime. One learns to enjoy and respect the power of powerful ideas" (p. 76). I want to convince you that podcasting can be a vehicle for teaching powerful ideas—not simply a new way to teach existing curriculum. My observations encourage me to think that student-powered podcasting can promote several powerful ideas—ideas that students can use over a lifetime. For example, the hands-on and reflective approach to copyright, fair use, and digital media that students employ in their podcasting can become a tool for them to think about the balance of individual rights and community benefits. Similarly, the powerful idea of audience, whether in creating a media review or an audio tour, can become a tool for them to empathize with and anticipate the needs of others. In student-powered podcasting, these issues are not isolated lessons, but fundamentals of students' work as podcasters.

New technologies do not necessarily lead to better teaching. I feel frustration when I see a tech-savvy and well-intentioned teacher, standing at the front of a class, cranking up a set of desktop speakers and playing a podcast that "enhances" the existing curriculum. Regardless of how compelling and polished the content is, if that's the extent of the technology integration, the teacher is most likely simply reinforcing passivity in the learners. On the other hand, I feel excitement when I see students empowered with creative technology tools that help them effectively participate in media creation, personal understanding, and communication with others.

Teach your students to podcast, and you'll take them further down the road to 21st-century literacy.

Works Cited

American Association of School Librarians (2007). Standards for the 21st-century learner. Retrieved November 12, 2008, from www.ala.org/ala/mgrps/divs/aasl/aaslproftools/learningstandards/ AASL_LearningStandards.pdf

Gee, J. P. (2004). *Situated language and learning: A critique of traditional schooling.* New York: Routledge.

Jenkins, H. (2006a). *Confronting the challenges of participatory culture: Media education for the 21st century.* Boston: MacArthur Foundation. Retrieved July 7, 2008, from http://newmedialiteracies.org/files/working/NMLWhitePaper.pdf

Jenkins, H. (2006b). *Convergence culture: Where old and new media collide.* New York: New York University Press.

Kist, W. (2004). *New literacies in action: Teaching and learning in multiple media* (Language and Literacy Series). New York: Teachers College Press.

Lankshear, C., & Knobel, M. (2006). *New literacies* (2nd ed., p. 272). Open University Press.

Papert, S. (1980). *Mindstorms: Children, computers, and powerful ideas.* New York: Basic Books.

Chapter 2

The Technologies of Podcasting

This chapter will give you an overview of the technologies of podcasting. The projects in the book address good teaching and learning, so they should be of interest to educators who are experienced podcasters as well as those who have no prior experience. If you are a newbie, you can begin shortly. Those who can operate a word processor and a tape recorder, and can add an attachment to an e-mail message, have 90% of the skills needed to become a skilled podcaster.

What Makes a Podcast?

There is both the core concept of podcasting that relates to the medium as well as an ever-changing array of specific technologies.

The core concept of podcasting is the distribution of media files in a series of "episodes." The term *podcast* can be used to refer to the individual episodes or to the entire series. This series of episodes is subscribable, portable, and can be consumed asynchronously. Before we review the specific technologies that you will use to create a podcast, let's look at the characteristics of this core concept. Let's look closely at the terms *media, episode, series, subscribable, portable,* and *asynchronous.*

Media. The traditional media used in podcasts has been audio files, but video podcasting (also known as vodcasting) is growing in popularity. The common file format for audio podcasts is the mp3 format; it is preferred because of its fidelity, relatively small file size, and interoperability.

Individual Episode versus Entire Series. Because a key distinction between a podcast and a standalone mp3 file on a website is the ability to subscribe and to get updates from a podcast, the series of media files completes the definition of a podcast. However, it is common to refer to a single episode within a series as a podcast as well.

Subscribable. The technology that makes a podcast subscribable is an RSS feed (RSS is generally agreed to stand for *Really Simple Syndication*). An RSS feed is a small file associated with podcast content that announces new episodes and episode information to everyone who has subscribed. People can subscribe to a podcast through a feed catcher (also called an aggregator or podcatcher). It's very easy to take advantage of RSS feeds.

An individual can subscribe to numerous feeds and be continually updated with a variety of content using a podcatcher. Currently, the most popular podcatcher is iTunes, the free, downloadable software from Apple. There are several other podcatchers available (e.g., Zune Marketplace, Juice). Most podcatchers are client software, meaning they are unique software programs that must be downloaded to your computer. There is, however, a burgeoning movement of Internet-based podcatchers, so keep on the lookout for those. Many aggregators not specifically dedicated to podcasts will let you subscribe and listen to podcasts (e.g., Bloglines and Google Reader), but these generic aggregators usually lack many of the advanced features of client software, such as the ability to automatically set and download files or to transfer them to portable players.

Portable. Another distinguishing feature of a podcast is its ability to be easily downloaded and played on portable devices, such as iPods, mp3 players, and cell phones.

Asynchronous. Podcasts are not intended to be distributed and consumed at the same time. Whether on a portable device or computer, they are intended to be consumed at the discretion of the consumer.

If you haven't already, go out and subscribe to some podcasts! There are podcasts available on almost any topic imaginable. You'll have much better luck understanding podcasting and teaching it to your students if you're familiar with some podcasting examples beforehand. Plus, it's fun!

Syndication

As I previously mentioned, a media file is not a true podcast unless it is syndicated, even if it's available on the Internet. You need to give your podcast the power of "subscribability" so listeners can receive it automatically in their podcatchers or other aggregators. There is a long and ever-changing list of options to achieve syndication, and no single one will fit everyone's needs. I will present some popular, inexpensive, and easy-to-use options.

Many schools use commercial content systems to run their websites. Increasingly, these content management systems are coming with podcasting components—specifically the ability to host media files such as mp3 files, to generate an RSS feed, and to index the series of podcasts on a website. I suggest exploring this option first.

If you do not have access to this application on your school's server, there are several free or inexpensive alternatives. These are sites that will host your media files and generate an RSS feed. Four popular ones are Blip.tv (www.blip.tv), Podomatic (www.podomatic.com), OurMedia (www.ourmedia.org) and Switchpod (www.switchpod.com). All of these services will create a single page for you that will archive your shows. In this way, listeners can access your podcast simply through a web browser without a subscription, or they can choose to subscribe.

Creating Audio Files

As we've discussed, part of what makes a podcast a podcast is its method of distribution, such as syndication via RSS feed. The other piece of the puzzle is how to create the media for distribution—in other words, how to create the individual episodes. In this book we'll mainly focus on audio, but I do include some information on video files as well.

The software that you will be working with is multitrack audio editing software. This software gives you the ability to collect audio from various sources (the Internet, CDs, your microphone, a portable device) and then purposefully mix it. The tracks are the individual sounds (narration, interviews, sound effects, music) that you will mix into a single audio file. (For example, one track might contain music and another track might contain an interview. You could then mix the tracks so the music plays as background to the interview.)

If you already know how to operate a tape recorder and a word processing program, you have 90% of the skills needed to learn multitrack audio editing. Three of the most popular audio editing programs are SourceForge's Audacity, Apple's GarageBand, and Adobe Audition. Audacity is a free download that works with Windows, Mac, or Linux operating systems; GarageBand works only on Macs and is a very intuitive program with a library of royalty-free sounds for mixing; Audition is a robust, professional product with many advanced features. Once you learn one kind of multitrack audio editing software, you will easily be able to learn others.

Coming up in Chapter 3 are two tutorials on audio editing: one for Audacity and one for GarageBand.

A Note on Video Podcast (Vodcast) File Formats

A video podcast, or vodcast, is simply a series of video files on the Internet with an associated RSS feed. There are many video file formats; however, if you want to syndicate a vodcast on iTunes, allowing people to play episodes on iPods, you will need to use one of the following video file formats: mp4 (mpeg4), m4v, or mov. These are files that are automatically generated by Apple video editing software such as QuickTime Pro, iMovie, or Final Cut Pro.

If you are using a PC, the two most common (and free) video authoring applications are Movie Maker and Photo Story. Both will export as Windows Media Video (wmv) files, which iTunes does not currently accept. However, if you want to syndicate your vodcast on iTunes and you have a PC, you do have a few options. You can purchase QuickTime Pro for your PC (about $30) or purchase another commercial software package that exports as mp4, m4v, or mov, or you can use a video conversion program to convert your files.

These video file conversion applications are a simple and inexpensive way to convert your vodcast episodes for iTunes. They will change your wmv files to mov files. Although I have never come across a genuine "freeware" version of these programs, many have trial versions that give you access to the software for a trial period, let you use the full program but leave a watermark on your converted video, or only allow for a short segment of video to be converted.

Despite my resistance to associating podcasting with commercial products, the popularity and convenience of iTunes (especially when used with an iPod) cannot be ignored. It would be misleading not to consider the hold that this software has on the podcasting phenomenon. Because of this influence I recommend indexing all podcasts and vodcasts on iTunes.

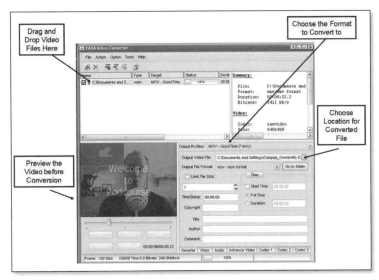

Figure 2.1 | YASA Video Converter

I used the trial version of YASA Video Converter (www.yasasoft.com) before purchasing. It converted to and from multiple file formats. The free trial version is limited to exporting videos of 5 minutes. Figure 2.1 shows an image of the YASA Video Converter. Almost all conversion programs work similarly.

Getting Meta

Metadata is information (data) about your podcast that will help people to find it when searching and to decide whether to subscribe. For example, here is the metadata for the Discovery News podcast:

> Stay on top of the latest developments in science news, including space exploration, technological breakthroughs, archaeological findings, animals, environmental research and more. Tags: news, science, environment, Discovery Channel, science news.

Title your podcast in an accurate but unique way, keeping in mind that most people will find your podcast via a search. A title such as "School Podcast" would make it difficult to distinguish. Also, take care to categorize your podcast accurately. Many people will browse through categories as they select podcasts to subscribe to. Include tags, or keywords. Most indexes and podcatchers will give show summaries and episode descriptions. Finally, consider including an image that can be associated with your podcast all the way to a portable device. Design or choose an image that can work well on a computer screen, cell phone, or mp3 player. Involve your students in the decision about which metadata to include.

Chapter 3

Audio Tutorials
and
Strategies

Following are two tutorials to teach you and your students the fundamental features of audio editing. The first tutorial focuses on the free software Audacity (for PCs and older Macs). The second tutorial focuses on the software GarageBand for the Mac.

Following the two tutorials, I discuss the essential elements of audio drama, and I provide an introduction to Foley art, the art of creating sound effects.

▶ TUTORIAL

Audacity Tutorial for PCs
(and Macs without GarageBand)

This tutorial will give you and your students a fundamental understanding of multitrack audio editing with Audacity. I have used it successfully to show students as well as teachers from kindergarten to graduate school how to use and teach with Audacity. You can follow this tutorial on your own or use it with your students. It will provide you and them with enough skill and knowledge to do a variety of projects with audio in your classroom.

THE SOFTWARE

Audacity is a free, cross-platform, open-source program that can be downloaded at http://audacity.sourceforge.net. It is a favorite of podcasters and digital audio enthusiasts because of its versatility and simplicity (and its price). After you have downloaded the software to your computer, all you need is a microphone, and you can create multitrack audio projects, save them as mp3s, and podcast them!

OVERVIEW

You are producing a podcast about the California Gold Rush. One aspect of the podcast is bringing to life the actual words of the people who participated in it. You base this episode on a letter from Lucius Fairchild, a young man from Madison, Wisconsin, who left home at age 18 to strike it rich in California in 1849. The letter comes from the Library of Congress American Memories Project.

You will record the narration of Fairchild's letter and then mix in sound effects and music. You will record one track (narration) and import two tracks (mining effects and music), edit them separately, mix them together, and export a finished file.

These instructions and resources are very specific. As you and your students become more familiar with the software and procedures, you can develop different projects and allow the students more choices and flexibility in their work.

The tutorial covers these basic skills for audio editing:

- Recording sounds
- Importing sounds

- Working with multiple audio tracks

- Looping sounds

- Shifting tracks

- Adding effects

- Exporting as an mp3 file

PROCEDURES

1. Download Audacity from http://audacity.sourceforge.net and install it on your computer. Additionally, download the LAME encoder file. This file is needed to convert files to mp3s and differs for Macs and PCs. Look for the link to the LAME encoder file on the Audacity website. Remember where you save the LAME file; you will be prompted for it in Step 12.

2. Download the music and sound effects at http://ccmixter.org/files/cs272/15786/. They are in a zipped file named cs272_-_Oh_My_Darling.zip. I created these sounds and you have complete permission to use them for this tutorial.

3. Record yourself or a student reading Fairchild's letter (see next page). Open up Audacity and go to File/New to start a new project. You should see a blank screen like this:

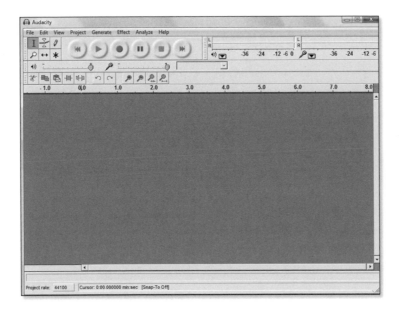

4. Click the record button and read the following letter into the microphone. (You may rehearse first if desired.)

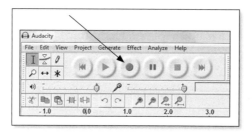

February 12, 1850

To J. C. Fairchild and Family,

…I think we are in the poorest diggings in the country and we have made as much this winter as any store in Madison can make in a year. About four weeks ago the river rose very high and drove us on the highest part of the bar where we supposed there was no gold of any consequence, but to our surprise we found it the richest part so we all took our ground and went to work, since that it has not rained and we have all done well. Ed & I have taken out *over Twelve hundred dollars* or over 2 ounces a day which is good wages…

I remain Your affectionate Friend, Son, & Brother

(From *California As I Saw It: First-Person Narratives of California's Early Years, 1849–1900*. The California Letters of Lucius Fairchild. Library of Congress American Memories Project. Retrieved January 4, 2006, from http://memory.loc.gov)

You should get something that looks like the following image. This is your first track.

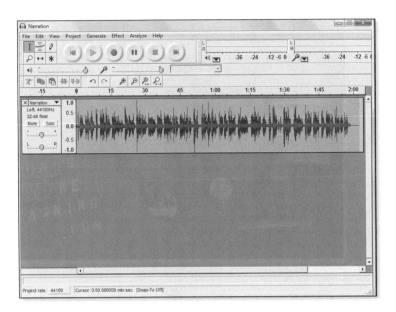

5. From the zipped file you downloaded in Step 2, extract the two audio files named Clementine.mp3 and Mining.mp3. Import them, one at a time, into your project by going to Project/Import/Audio.

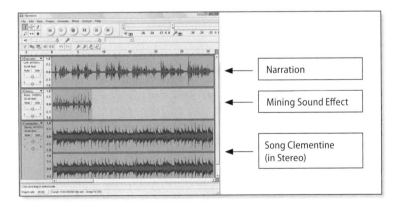

6. Experiment with playing a single track or combination of tracks by using the Mute and Solo buttons on each track's control panel. You can also move, rename, and do other actions to the tracks by clicking the top bar of the control panel.

7. We will now manipulate the individual tracks. First, we will loop the mining sound effect so that it repeatedly plays throughout the recording. Second, we will arrange the music and sound effects so that they both start before the narration. Third, we will make the music and sound effects louder before the narration and quieter during the narration. (Note: To do any editing your clip must be stopped, not paused.) You will work with the Selection and Time Shift Tools:

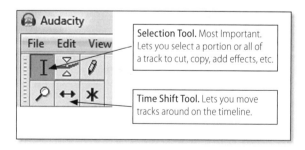

8. Looping a track means replaying it over and over to seamlessly convey a continuous sound. To loop the mining track, select it using the Selection tool, copy it, and then paste it on the track right next to the original selection. Repeat this duplication until the mining track goes about 10 seconds beyond the narration track. The bottom of the toolbar has a timeline in seconds. You may have to go to View/Zoom Out to get a better view of all the tracks.

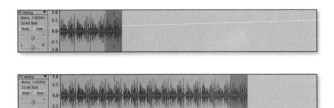

9. We will use the time shift tool to move the narration forward 10 seconds. Make sure your recording is stopped. Click the Time Shift tool in the top right of your screen. Drag the narration forward ten seconds.

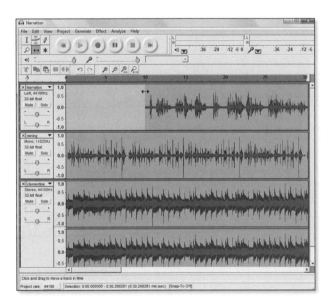

You may click the Play button on the top of the screen at any time to hear your creation.

10. Now we are going to lower the volume on the mining sound effects and music tracks when the narration track is playing. We will lower the volume on the mining track first. Using the Selection tool, highlight the section of the mining track that is concurrent with the narration. Then go to Effect/Amplify and lower the amplification by 2.5 decibels (–2.5 dB). You can experiment with the exact levels based on the recording of your narration. (Along with amplification, you can add a variety of other effects such as echo, changing the pitch, or changing the speed of a selected section of track.)

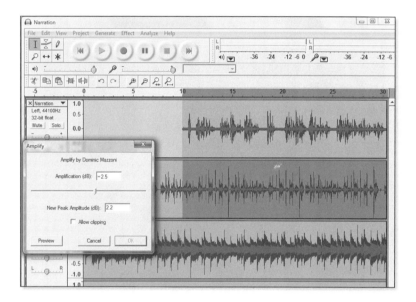

Repeat these steps to lower the volume with the Clementine track. Play the entire audio project. Make minor adjustments to taste.

11. Your final project should look something like this:

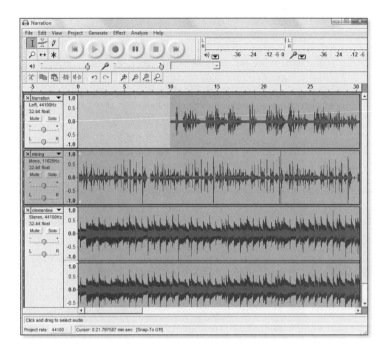

12. Before exporting your project, first save it as an Audacity file (.aup is the extension). This file type will keep all of the tracks and effects distinct so you can go back and edit the Audacity project if you need to. Now we will export the file as an mp3. Go to the File menu and choose Export As MP3.

The first time you export an mp3 file you will be prompted to tell Audacity where the LAME Encoder file is. Just point the prompt to where you downloaded the file (see Step 1):

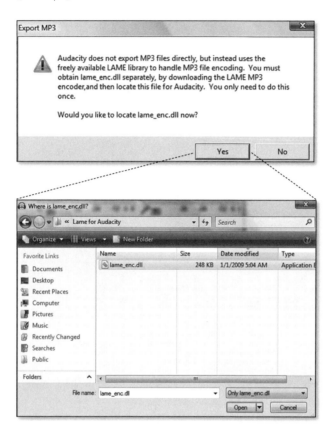

EXAMPLES

You may hear finished examples of this tutorial here:

http://podcourse.blogspot.com/2007/03/audacity-tutorial-audacity-tutorial-was.html

 ▶ TUTORIAL

GarageBand Tutorial for Macs

By Jeff Humphrey

This tutorial will give you and your students a fundamental understanding of multitrack audio editing with GarageBand. I have used it successfully to show students as well as teachers from kindergarten to graduate school how to use and teach multitrack audio recording with GarageBand. You can follow this tutorial on your own or use it with your students. It will provide you and them with enough skill and knowledge to do a variety of projects with audio in your classroom.

This tutorial is similar to the previous one, except it uses GarageBand rather than Audacity. If you have a Mac OS with GarageBand, I would recommend that software for creating your podcasts. If your Mac OS does not include GarageBand, there is a version of Audacity you can use (see the Audactiy tutorial).

THE SOFTWARE

GarageBand is a program that's included in Apple's iLife software package and often comes bundled with the OS X operating system. This program is popular among musicians and podcasters alike. GarageBand is a powerful multitrack audio recording and editing tool. It contains many features you would expect to find in professional audio applications, but the interface is extremely user-friendly, well laid out, and intuitive. The following tutorial was created for GarageBand '08.

OVERVIEW

You are producing a podcast about the California Gold Rush. One aspect of the podcast is bringing to life the actual words of the people who participated in it. You base this episode on a letter from Lucius Fairchild, a young man from Madison, Wisconsin, who left home at age 18 to strike it rich in California in 1849. The letter comes from the Library of Congress American Memories Project.

You will record the narration of Fairchild's letter and then mix in sound effects and music. You will record one track (narration) and import two tracks (mining effects and music), edit them separately, mix them together, and export a finished file.

These instructions and resources are very specific. As you and your students become more familiar with the software and procedures, you can develop different projects and allow the students more choices and flexibility in their work.

The tutorial covers these basic skills for audio editing:

- Using GarageBand's podcast template
- Recording sounds
- Importing sounds
- Working with multiple audio tracks
- Working with regions
- Looping sounds
- Shifting tracks
- Adding effects
- Exporting your podcast

INTRODUCTION TO THE GARAGEBAND WINDOW

The GarageBand window contains five sections:

1. **The Track Mixer:** displays the individual audio tracks in your session. There are controls for volume and panning (sound distribution between the right and left speaker) as well as volume meters for monitoring each track's volume level. This is the main window. The four windows listed next can be toggled on and off as needed.

2. **The Editor:** where editing is performed for audio tracks and where information about your episode can be added on a podcast track.

3. **The Loop Browser:** used to locate and import prerecorded music and sound effect loops included with GarageBand.

4. **The Media Browser:** used to locate and import media files from iTunes, iMovie, and iPhoto.

5. Track Info: contains basic information about the track and provides access to audio effects.

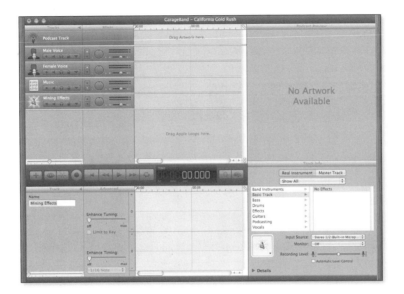

In the podcast template there are five tracks set up for you. The male and female voice tracks contain preset effects to enhance your voice, depending on gender.

PROCEDURES

1. Download the music and sound effects at http://ccmixter.org/files/cs272/15786/. They are in a zipped file named cs272_-_Oh_My_Darling.zip. From the zipped file, extract the two audio files Clementine.mp3 and Mining.mp3. You have complete permission to use these sounds for this tutorial.

2. Open GarageBand and select Create New Podcast Episode. This template is set up specifically for podcast production. To customize the template for the purpose of this project, do the following:

   a. Create a new track by selecting Track/New Basic Track. This track will be named No Effects by default.

b. Toggle between the Track Editor and Track Info windows to rename the tracks. In the Track Info window, rename the No Effects track to "Mining Effects." Then select the Jingles track in the Track Editor and rename it to "Music" in the Track Info window.

c. You may change the instrument icon on your Mining Effects track in the Track Info window.

3. To prepare to record the narration, click on the Record Enable button on either the Male or Female Voice track as appropriate.

4. Now click Record on the Transport Controls below and begin reading the letter below into the microphone (you may rehearse first if desired).

February 12, 1850

To J. C. Fairchild and Family,

…I think we are in the poorest diggings in the country and we have made as much this winter as any store in Madison can make in a year. About four weeks ago the river rose very high and drove us on the highest part of the bar where we supposed there was no gold of any consequence, but to our surprise we found it the richest part so we all took our ground and went to work, since that it has not rained and we have all done well. Ed & I have taken out *over Twelve hundred dollars* or over 2 ounces a day which is good wages…

I remain Your affectionate Friend, Son, & Brother

(From *California As I Saw It: First-Person Narratives of California's Early Years, 1849–1900*. The California Letters of Lucius Fairchild. Library of Congress American Memories Project. Retrieved January 4, 2006, from http://memory.loc.gov/)

5. You will see your audio being recorded as you are speaking. It will look like this:

Remember that any stutters, dead air, or the like can be edited out later. It's a good idea to click the Record Enable button on your Voice track so that it is not red. This will prevent you from accidentally recording over a track. You may also click the Lock/Unlock button, which will prevent any inadvertent changes to your track.

6. Drag the extracted Clementine.mp3 and Mining.mp3 files (see Step 1) to their respective tracks in the GarageBand window. The Music and Mining Effects tracks will now be populated with the audio you just imported. These clips are called *regions*.

7. The Mining Effects region is not as long as the music or narration regions. In order to lengthen it, we will use looping. Place your mouse pointer on the upper right-hand corner of the Mining Effects region. The pointer changes into a circular arrow called the loop pointer. Click and hold the mouse button and, using the loop pointer, drag your region as far to the right as you want it to play. You will notice notches that appear in the top and bottom of the region. These represent each complete loop created.

GarageBand Regions

Each time you record or import audio, the resulting audio clip is called a region. You can think of regions as independent chunks of audio. Regions can be edited, shifted, reordered, and looped. Imported regions are orange; recorded regions are purple.

8. Now we will use the Track Editor to edit your voice track.

Select your voice track by clicking on it. Now open the Track Editor by clicking the button that has the scissors on it. You will see your region in the Track Editor window. There is a zoom level control in the bottom left corner of the Track Editor. By sliding the control to the right, you can zoom into your track to see more detail.

If there is a stutter or dead air in your narration, you can highlight it by clicking and holding down the mouse button and dragging the cursor over the portion of the track you'd like to delete. Once the area is highlighted, choose Edit/Cut. Now there are two regions with a gap in between them.

9. After deleting part of your voice track, you will want to remove any gaps between the regions. This is done by clicking and dragging the regions in the main window.

10. Shift-click on each region in the track and choose Edit/Join. This will merge the separate regions back together into one piece. (Merging the regions will come in handy later if you decide to shift the entire track forwards or backwards. It's easier to shift one contiguous region than multiple separate regions.)

11. Once your narration editing is complete, shift the narration region about 15 seconds forward by clicking and dragging. Use the ruler above the tracks as a guide. You will be left with a 15-second introduction of music and sound effects before the narration begins.

12. Now it's time to mix your project. The main concern is adjusting the volume of each track to an appropriate level. You're going to want to lower the volume of the music and mining effects for the duration of the narration. To do this, click on the Show Track Volume button on both the Mining Effects and Music tracks. A graphical representation of the track's volume will appear below the track. By clicking on the blue line, you will create a breakpoint. The breakpoint can be moved up or down to raise or lower the track's volume.

Create a breakpoint in both tracks just before the narration begins. Try lowering the volume of both tracks by 3 dB (decibels). Create a second breakpoint at the end of the narration and raise the volume of the effects and music back to their original levels. You may want to experiment with different volume levels depending on the volume level of your narration.

13. One of the most useful features in GarageBand podcast production is the podcast track. It is always the uppermost track in the main window. The podcast track allows you to easily add artwork, notes, and episode information to your podcast (metadata; see p. 18). By selecting the podcast track, an information window will open where you can add this information.

14. Now you are ready to create your podcast file. Click on the Share menu at the top of the window to see the list of options. Send Podcast to iTunes will export your finished podcast directly to your iTunes library. Export Podcast to Disk will allow you to save your podcast file to a specified location on your hard drive. If you have an iWeb account, you can choose Send Podcast to iWeb and it will be exported and published.

EXAMPLES

You can hear finished examples of this tutorial here:

http://podcourse.blogspot.com/2007/03/audacity-tutorial-audacity-tutorial-was.html

EXTENSION

There are a variety of special audio effects built into GarageBand such as echo and equalization. Select the narration track and click the Show Track Info button. You will notice a list of instrument categories on the left side of the Track Info window. Select Vocals.

A list of preset effects will appear on the right. Try selecting different presets from the list to add different special effects to your narration.

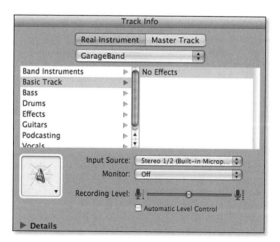

On the bottom of the Track Info window you will see manual controls for each of the audio effects.

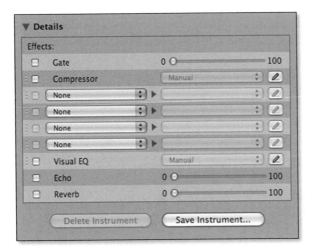

If you want to learn more, there is lots of great information in GarageBand Help that will describe each effect in detail. Feel free to experiment with effects. It can be a lot of fun.

Elements of Audio Drama

The beginning units in this book focus on creating a variety of audio dramas. While each project is unique, there are consistent elements of an audio drama that you should think about and focus on with your students. These elements are:

- Music

- Sound effects

- Narration (tells the story and explains the action)

- Dialogue (what the characters say to each other)

When you create an audio drama, you have several tools to tell your story. You can use dialogue (conversations among people), narration (a person telling the story), music, and sound effects. Most good audio dramas will use some effective combination of these techniques. Have your students listen to these very different audio dramas from Drama Pod with an ear for those four elements. You can simply play the first two minutes of each to see the different combination of elements in action.

- Star Trek—Lost Frontier, Episode 7: Resistance
  www.dramapod.com/episodes.php?catid=219&start=3

- Clever Gretel—Fairy Tale Corner 019
  www.dramapod.com/episodes.php?catid=309

What did you notice about each audio drama? How does each show use music, sound effects, narration, and dialogue differently?

Foley Art: Creating Sound Effects

Throughout the book there is a focus on legally and ethically using music and sound effects from existing sources. If you or your students are musically inclined, you should also consider including original music. Moreover, there is one area that I would like to emphasize as educationally worthwhile for all students—creating original sound effects. The process of creating sound effects for movies and radio is often referred to as Foley art, named for Jack Foley, one of the pioneers of the practice.

Figure 3.1 | Foley art is the art of sound effects.

There are numerous educational benefits to doing Foley art in classrooms. First of all, students and teachers love it. It's fun, and it stretches the imagination when household items are utilized to create sound effects for audio dramas. Besides being enjoyable, Foley art captures an important lesson about the importance of mediums. It strongly illustrates the point that, in audio, what we see is irrelevant—it is what we hear that matters. Audio is a powerful medium because it demands that a listener act as a collaborator in the production—supplying the pictures for what is heard. This is no more apparent than when a breaking celery stick becomes a cracking bone or the rap of coconuts on a table becomes a galloping horse.

The ability to manipulate and create fictional worlds from disparate sources is a process that students should learn to ethically and effectively participate in and identify. As teachers and students use these Foley techniques in their classrooms, attention and discussion should focus on when and when not to use them. Why is it acceptable to use Foley techniques in an audio drama? Why wouldn't it be acceptable in a news report?

Finally, students can participate in communities of practice, such as the Free Sound Project (www.freesound.org) and Soungle (www.soungle.com), as they contribute, share, and comment on sounds in communities of likeminded audiophiles.

Below is a scene adapted from Macbeth (Act 3, Scene 3) that works well with Foley techniques. Your students do not need to be familiar with the play to enjoy producing this scene.

Macbeth—Act 3, Scene 3

[A park near the palace.]

Enter three Murderers wait to kill Banquo and Fleance.
The First and Second Murderer were not expecting the Third Murderer.

First Murderer:
But who did bid thee join with us?

Third Murderer:
Macbeth.

Second Murderer:
He needs not our mistrust, since he delivers
Our offices and what we have to do
To the direction just.

First Murderer:
Then stand with us.
The west yet glimmers with some streaks of day.

Third Murderer:
Hark! I hear horses.

When converting the above scene from a stage production to an audio production, you can use Foley effects for both the stated and implied stage direction. You can add footsteps for the "Enter three Murderers" and galloping horses for the implied sound effect in "Hark! I hear horses."

The stated stage directions of the murderers entering can be done by having two to three students crunch potato chips in a bowl with their hands. (I suggest having students wear latex gloves—students enjoy the process of putting them on and they prevent their hands from getting greasy from the chips). You can have the students rehearse and discuss the effects of various decisions. Do the murderers enter at the same time? Do they run fast or slow? What are the artistic and emotional effects of the different choices on the listening audience?

Similarly, you can add sound effects with the implied stage directions for the sound of horses galloping with cut coconut shells. You can have two students each use two coconut shells and tap them on different surfaces. You can also discuss the effect on the audience of having fast or slow horses.

Often, students will decide on beginning the scene with two murderers entering slowly and then one quickly crunching behind and ending the scene with the tense sound of two quickly galloping horses. You can add music as an introduction or background to the scene as well.

You can see a video demonstration of students doing the Foley work for this scene at www.folger.edu/template.cfm?cid=2614/.

Here are some examples of other Foley techniques:

- Army marching: boots on wood, repeated and looped

- Shovels: spoons in sand or pebbles

- Applause: two to three people clapping, repeated and looped

- Knocking on door: knocking on desk or wood

- Time bomb ticking: clock

- Airplane engine: fan starting and running

- Helicopter: opening and closing an umbrella very fast

- Bones breaking: cracking celery or carrots

- Knight moving in armor: set of keys jingling

- Walking in snow: patting cornstarch

- Dinosaur, monster, or large animal eating: chewing watermelon

- Elevator door closing: closing a desk drawer or filing cabinet

- Boiling water: blowing bubbles in water with straw

Section II
Podcasting Units

All of the following units involve audio recording—students recording themselves performing a scene, giving an interview, reading poetry, providing commentary, and so forth. The individual unit procedures do not cover the specifics of how to record a podcast and use music and sound effects—please review Chapter 3 for this information. See the rubric at the end of each unit for the standards addressed in that unit.

Unit 1

"I've Been Waiting for You"
Radio Drama

This activity is adapted from the Folger Shakespeare Library's Shakespeare Set Free Teaching Workshop. In the workshop, a word such as "Oh," a phrase such as "I ate the sandwich," or a short scene such as the one in this project is given to students, but with various contexts. For example, one student will be asked to say "Oh" as if she won the lottery and another will say it as if he stubbed his toe; or a student will have to say "I ate the sandwich" emphasizing the word "I," and another student will say the phrase emphasizing the word "sandwich." The workshop teaches the connection between text and context and is an introduction to more complex situations in which a character's or a person's language conveys extra meaning, subtext, or irony—such as Iago's language in *Othello*.

This unit also teaches the attributes of different media as well as citation procedures. Students will experience the attributes of different mediums—live performance and audio production—as creators and audience members. Understanding the unique possibilities, strengths, and limitations of the medium of audio will lay a foundation for the rest of the podcasting units.

SUMMARY

In this activity student pairs will each create a unique short radio drama using the same seven lines of dialogue. Students will make their own drama unique by taking on specific characters, using tone and inflection, using sound effects and music, and writing narration.

GRADE LEVELS

Grades 5–12

OBJECTIVES

- To examine the role of context on situations and language
- To explore the unique aspects of audio
- To internalize the process of ethically using the intellectual property of others to create original content

TIME ALLOWANCE

2–5 days

RESOURCES

At least one computer with multitrack audio editing software and a microphone

Procedures

Organize your classroom into groups of two and distribute Unit 1, Worksheet 1 to every student pair. If you have an odd number of students, you can make a few groups of three and give one student the role of director. Tell each pair that they have to enact—in front of the class—this dialogue:

Person 1: I've been waiting for you.

Person 2: I'm sorry I'm late.

Person 1: That's OK.

Person 2: Thank you.

Person 1: I have something for you.

Person 2: What is it?

Person 1: This.

Then give each pair one of the following roles: gangsters, snobs, spies, husband and wife, teacher and student, child and parent, robots, pet store clerks, aliens, burglars, police officers, movie stars, detective and suspect, best friends, long-lost friends, or whatever else you can think up. You can repeat roles for large classes. Allow students 5–10 minutes for rehearsals and encourage them to imaginatively use props from the classroom. Unit 1, Worksheet 2 can help students focus and organize their entire production.

After the classroom productions, describe and contrast the audio scene that they will now do. How will they convey their roles without physical actions or props? What resources unique to audio will they be able to use? One key element is how they will convey the "This" at the end of the scene.

For the audio scene, give each pair the same roles (gangsters, snobs, etc.) and have them write an introductory and concluding narrative. Describe how they can use inflection, tone, narration, sound effects, and music. Explain Creative Commons (from Appendix A) and have them use music from the Creative Commons Mixter (www.ccmixter.org) and sound effects from The Free Sounds Project (www.freesound.org).

Have students record and mix their scenes. At the end of the scene, students should cite the audio files that they used, giving enough information so that listeners can find the information themselves. I typically give the students a citation script like the one below.

> The music for this project came from the Creative Commons Mixter **<<Say Original File Name(s)>>** with a **<<Say Type of License>>**.

> The sound effects for this project came from the Free Sounds Project **<<Say Original File Name(s)>>**. All sound effects have a Creative Commons Sampling 1.0 Plus license.

Examples

You can hear examples of student work here—a detective and a suspect, a school principal and student, an English husband and wife, and two pairs of gangsters:

http://podcourse.blogspot.com/2007/04/audio-theater-1.html

Rubric for Unit 1: "I've Been Waiting for You" Radio Drama

	Exemplary	Satisfactory	Unacceptable
Narration	Narration describes the actions of the characters and the situation before and after the dialogue in clear and standard English	Narration describes the actions of the characters before and after dialogue but is occasionally unclear or nonstandard English	Little/no narration or narration is inappropriate for play (language choice or length)
Dialogue	Consistent attempt to portray both characters with given dialogue	Some but inconstant attempt to portray both characters with given dialogue	No/little attempt to portray characters *or* changes in dialogue
Music	Appropriate to play and mixed to complement voices	Appropriate music during play but sound levels occasionally interfere with voices	No music or inappropriate choice or use of music
Sound Effects	Appropriate to play and enhance the overall experience	Appropriate sound effects but interfere with overall listening experience	No or inappropriate sound effects
Citations of Music and Sound Effects Resources	Clear credit of resources in audio file from appropriate sources—listener can easily find source material, Creative Commons material, or student can justify fair use	Attempt to credit resources used, audio and resources are from appropriate sources—Creative Commons material or student can justify fair use	No citations of audio or inappropriate audio used or student unable to justify fair use
Legal and Ethical Guidelines	All course rules are followed consistently through the process	Course rules are followed for final production, but minor deviations occur during process	Repeated or significant violations of course rule throughout process

(continued)

Rubric for Unit 1: "I've Been Waiting for You" Radio Drama *(continued)*

	Related NETS·S	Related IRA/NCTE Standards	Related AASL Standards	Related TESOL Standards	Related WIDA Standards
Narration	1.a, 1.b, 5.a, 6.a, 6.b	3, 4, 5, 8		3.1, 3.3	1—Speaking 1—Writing
Dialogue	1.a, 1.b, 5.a, 6.a, 6.b	3, 4, 8		1.1, 3.1	1—Speaking
Music	1.a, 1.b, 5.a, 6.a, 6.b	3, 8	1.2.2, 1.2.3, 4.3.2		
Sound Effects	1.a, 1.b, 5.a, 6.a, 6.b	3, 8	1.2.2, 1.2.3, 4.3.2		
Citations of Music and Sound Effects Resources	3.b, 5.a	4, 8	1.3.1, 1.3.3, 1.3.5, 3.1.6, 4.3.4		1—Speaking 1—Writing
Legal and Ethical Guidelines	5.a, 6.a		1.3.1, 1.3.3, 1.3.5, 3.1.6, 4.3.4		

Unit 2

Reader's Theater

Reader's Theater is a popular instructional approach in which students read a scripted version of a book or story. Reader's Theater is characterized by minimal props, costumes, or sets; reading as opposed to memorizing the scripts; and an inclusive approach to student participation. Reader's Theater motivates students to engage in texts and repeated readings, and it improves fluency and comprehension.

By adding creative elements of digital audio, you can simultaneously enhance the fluency and comprehension of the students as well as introduce new creative and meaning-making skills. This unit addresses younger students and can be modified for students in Grades 2–5; the next unit, "*The Metamorphosis*: Audio Play Scripting," takes the same procedures but scales them up for older students by introducing more complex skills and decision making. Look at the unit below as an example of what you can do to various works of fiction in Grades 2–5.

SUMMARY

Students create an audio play from a script the teacher prepares from a prose story. Both the prose version and the script are provided as a model for transforming a story into a readers' theater performance script. Students read the prose version and then record their performance of the script, including narration, sound effects, and music. You can modify the number of narrators to suit your class or groups. For this unit you might want to review the ideas from Chapter 3, Elements of Radio Drama with your students.

GRADE LEVELS

Grades 2–5

OBJECTIVES

- Develop reading fluency
- Engage an audience with a creative work
- Use the material of others effectively and ethically

TIME ALLOWANCE

3–5 days

RESOURCES

At least one computer with multitrack audio editing software and a microphone

The frog ribbit sound effect may be downloaded here:
http://freesound.iua.upf.edu/samplesViewSingle.php?id=50406
(you will have to register for this site.)

Five music files may be downloaded here:
http://ccmixter.org/files/cs272/14300

Procedures

1. The teacher passes out Unit 2, Worksheet 1 to all students and assigns roles.

2. Students record their performance of the script, enacting all of the voices in the dialogue.

3. Students create three original sound effects—whistling, footsteps, and knocking at a door—and insert them at appropriate places in the performance.

4. Students insert an existing sound effect—frog ribbit—at the appropriate places.

5. Students choose a musical clip to play at the beginning and ending of the scene, before and after the narration and dialogue.

6. Students use multitrack audio editing software to mix all of these audio clips together into one track.

7. Students cite all of their sources.

The Ungrateful Son—Prose Version

This is the prose version that was used to create the performance script.

A husband and wife were once sitting by the door of their house, and they had a roasted chicken set before them and were about to eat it together. The husband said, "Mmm. This chicken looks good," and the wife replied, "Yes, it certainly does." Soon they heard the sound of a person whistling. The husband said, "Here comes my father down the road, look through the window and see him. Let's hide this chicken in the closet." There was then the sound of the father's footsteps and a knock at the door. The father came in and took a drink. The father said, "Thanks for the water. See you soon." The Father left. The son went to get the roasted chicken from the closet. When he grabbed it, it turned into a giant frog that jumped onto the man's face. The frog made a loud "RIBBIT."

The Husband was angry, "What happened to my chicken? What is this frog doing on my face?" The frog made another ribbit sound. The frog stayed on the man's face forever. If any one wanted to take it off, it looked venomously at the person, as if it would jump on his or her face. No one dared to touch it. When the man walked down the street a neighbor said, "Oh boy, that frog looks pretty mean. I don't want him on my face. Keep away from me!" And the ungrateful son was forced to feed the frog every day.

The Ungrateful Son—Performance Script

Roles: 12 Narrators, Husband, Wife, Neighbor, Father

Narrator 1:	A husband and his wife were once sitting by the door of their house.
Narrator 2:	And they had a roasted chicken set before them and were about to eat it together.
Husband:	Mmm. This chicken looks good.
Wife:	Yes, it certainly does.

[*Sound effect: whistling*]

Husband:	Here comes my father down the road. Look through the window and see him. Let's hide this chicken in the closet.

[*Sound effects: footsteps and knocking at door*]

Narrator 3:   The father came in and took a drink.

Father: Thanks for the water. See you soon.

Narrator 4:   The father left.

Narrator 5:   The son went to get the roasted chicken from the closet.

Narrator 6:   When he grabbed it, it turned into a giant frog...

Narrator 7:   ...that jumped on the man's face.

[*Sound effect: frog ribbit*]

Husband:
(Angry)   What happened to my chicken? What is this frog doing on my face?

[*Sound effect: frog ribbit*]

Narrator 8:   The frog stayed on the man's face forever.

Narrator 9:   If any one wanted to take it off, it looked venomously at the person, as if it would jump on his or her face.

Narrator 10:   No one dared to touch it.

Narrator 11:   When the man walked down the street a neighbor said,

Neighbor: Oh boy, that frog looks pretty mean. I don't want him on my face. Keep away from me!

Narrator 12:   And the ungrateful son was forced to feed the frog every day.

Example

Listen to a student example here:

http://podcourse.blogspot.com/2008/07/reader-theater-sequel.html.

Rubric for Unit 2: Reader's Theater

	Exemplary	Satisfactory	Unacceptable
Narrator Voice	Clearly tells the story	Most of the voice is clear	No narration, missing narration, or inaudible narration
Dialogue	Each voice is clearly heard, unique, and appropriate	Generally audible, voices do not fit characters	Inaudible or no/little changes in voices or inappropriate voices
Original Sound Effects	All three original sounds can be easily identified and are at the appropriate places	Two of the three sound effects are easily identifiable	One or none of the sounds are easily identifiable
Existing Sound Effects	Existing sound of frog ribbit is at the appropriate places	Frog ribbit is close to the appropriate places	Frog ribbit is in the wrong places or not present
Musical Introduction and Conclusion	One of the given sound files is at the beginning and end of the audio play	Music is at the introduction or conclusion, but not both. Music is one of the selected songs	Music is not from one of the song choices or missing from beginning and end
Mixing	All sounds tracks are at appropriate volume levels	All of the sound elements are generally audible, with some problems	Major volume problems with the different tracks
Citations of Music and Sound Effects Resources	Clear credit of resources in audio file from appropriate sources—listener can easily find source material, Creative Commons material, or student can justify fair use	Attempt to credit resources used, audio and resources are from appropriate sources—Creative Commons material or student can justify fair use	No citations of audio or inappropriate audio used or student unable to justify fair use
Legal and Ethical Guidelines	All course rules are followed consistently through the process	Course rules are followed for final production, but minor deviations occur during process	Repeated or significant violations of course rule throughout process

(continued)

Rubric for Unit 2: Reader's Theater *(continued)*

	Related NETS·S	Related IRA/NCTE Standards	Related AASL Standards	Related TESOL Standards	Related WIDA Standards
Narrator Voice	1.a, 1.b, 2.a, 6.a, 6.b, 6.d	1, 2, 3, 4, 5	1.1.6, 2.1.5, 2.1.6, 3.2.3, 4.1.3	1.1, 1.3, 2.1, 2.2, 2.3, 3.1	1, 2—Speaking 1, 2—Reading
Dialogue	1.a, 1.b, 2.a, 6.a, 6.b, 6.d	1, 2, 3, 4, 5	1.1.6, 2.1.5, 2.1.6, 3.2.3, 4.1.3	1.1, 1.3, 2.1, 2.2, 2.3, 3.1	1, 2—Speaking 1, 2—Reading
Original Sound Effects	1.a, 1.b, 2.a, 6.a, 6.b, 6.d	1, 2, 3, 4, 5	1.2.1, 2.1.5, 2.1.6, 3.2.3, 4.1.3, 4.3.2		
Existing Sound Effects	1.a, 1.b, 2.a, 6.a, 6.b, 6.d	1, 2, 3, 4, 5	1.2.1, 2.1.5, 2.1.6, 3.2.3, 4.1.3, 4.3.2		
Musical Introduction and Conclusion	1.a, 1.b, 2.a, 6.a, 6.b, 6.d	1, 2, 3, 4, 5	1.2.1, 2.1.5, 2.1.6, 3.2.3, 4.1.3, 4.3.2		
Mixing	1.a, 1.b, 2.a, 6.a, 6.b, 6.d	1, 2, 3, 4, 5	1.2.1, 2.1.5, 2.1.6, 3.2.3, 4.1.3, 4.3.2		
Citations of Music and Sound Effects Resources	3.b, 5.a	4, 8	1.3.1, 1.3.3, 1.3.5, 3.1.6, 4.3.4		1—Speaking 1—Writing
Legal and Ethical Guidelines	5.a, 6.a		1.3.1, 1.3.3, 1.3.5, 3.1.6, 4.3.4		

Unit 3

By Kate Mazzetti

The Metamorphosis:
Audio
Play Scripting

Creating an audio play can be the main focus of a literary unit, or it can be one of a series of activities that explores the transmission of a story through various mediums. In the case of the example used here, Kafka's *The Metamorphosis*, there have been stage plays, film adaptations, and a ballet that can stimulate a discussion of the attributes, differences, and strength of various media. This project can also be done even before students begin to study a piece of literature as a "teaser" or anticipatory set.

Regardless of how you incorporate them, creating audio plays is an especially rewarding experience—creatively and educationally—when students themselves adapt the prose of a novel to create an audio scene. In this process they need to consider issues of media, audience, and literary interpretation. This project goes beyond the production of audio and scaffolds and leads students in the thoughtful transformation of media—from prose to audio play.

Bedroom Door by Tony Platt. Used with permission.

The Metamorphosis offers another interesting dimension for English-speaking students in that it was originally written in German. Looking at, comparing, and combining various translations found online can be another aspect of this project. This unit would work well with works in the public domain such as *The Scarlet Letter, Moby Dick,* "The Yellow Wallpaper," and *Winesburg, Ohio.*

Feel free to use this unit, model it, modify it, and create your own. You might want to review the ideas from Chapter 3, Elements of Audio Drama with your students.

SUMMARY

Students adapt the prose of a novel to an audio play, considering issues of media, audience, and literary interpretation. As an example, this unit contains a readily-adaptable scene from *The Metamorphosis.*

GRADE LEVELS

Grades 6–12

OBJECTIVES

- Select printed text that can transfer to the medium of audio

- Transform printed literature into an audio script

- Produce an audio scene to engage a particular audience

- Use the material of others effectively and ethically

TIME ALLOWANCE

3–7 days

RESOURCES

At least one computer with multitrack audio editing software and a microphone

Procedures

There are three parts to this unit:

1. Choosing the text

2. Transforming literature into an audio scene script

3. Producing the final audio scene

During these steps, there are various issues to consider. Consider the following issues and use the questions to guide your discussions with students during their decision-making process.

Choosing the Text

When choosing an excerpt to produce with students, discuss the attributes that would make a compelling audio play. When would a good text for reading make a good play for an audio drama? When wouldn't it?

Transforming Literature into an Audio Scene Script

Narration. In the scene shown in this unit (Unit 3, Worksheet 1), some of the narrator's lines are taken directly from the novel, other lines from the novel are eliminated, and some become stage directions. What are the criteria for creating the narrator's spoken lines? When should students consider deleting or converting the narrator's words?

Adding Lines. In this version lines were added that were not in the novel. For example, the struggle that Gregor experiences to get out of bed and come to terms with his new insect body was turned into added lines of dialogue: "How did I get all of these legs? If I could just move this big belly of mine and get off the bed. Ouch!" When is it acceptable or even desirable to add dialogue? What arguments can be made not to add new lines of dialogue?

Adding Stage Directions. All of the stage directions were generated from the narrator of the novel or inferred from the lines. For example, the novel reads, "Gregor had a shock as he heard his own voice … unmistakably his own voice, it was true, but with a horrible twittering squeak behind it like an undertone." This was converted to the stage direction "speaking in a squeaky bug voice."

Paraphrasing. In many of the previous decisions, a certain amount of paraphrasing was done. One area worth discussing is the advantages and drawbacks of paraphrasing, particularly with figurative or poetic language or with antiquated words. For example, the text of the novel uses the term "fretwork," which means decorative carving in wood or metal. Although an option would have been to change the term to "carving" or "woodworking" to make the term more understandable to an American audience, students should consider the poetic and historic powers of unusual terms such as that. What is gained and lost when words are replaced and lines paraphrased?

Producing the Final Audio Scene

1. The teacher passes out Unit 3, Worksheet 1 to all students and assigns roles.

2. Students record their performance of the script, enacting all of the voices in the dialogue.

3. Students create original sound effects and insert them at appropriate places in the performance.

4. Students choose a musical clip to play at the beginning and ending of the scene, before and after the narration and dialogue.

5. Students use multitrack audio editing software to mix all of these audio clips together into one track.

6. Students cite all of their sources.

Example

http://podcourse.blogspot.com/2009/04/metamorphosis.html

Rubric for Unit 3: *The Metamorphosis:* Audio Play Scripting

	Exemplary	Satisfactory	Unacceptable
Selection	Excerpt makes compelling listening on its own	Excerpt is generally interesting with some confusion out of context	Excerpt is uninteresting and is incomprehensible out of context of the novel or short story
Transformation *(should be assessed in conference with students)*	Process of adaptation consistently considered issues of adding, removing, and paraphrasing material	Process of adaptation generally considered issues of adding, removing, and paraphrasing material	Process of adaptation seldom considered issues of adding, removing, and paraphrasing material
Production	Dialogue, music, and sound effects worked seamlessly well together	Dialogue, music, and sound effects generally worked together	Dialogue, music, and sound effects did not work well together
Citations of Music and Sound Effects Resources	Clear credit of resources in audio file from appropriate sources—listener can easily find source material, Creative Commons material, or student can justify fair use	Attempt to credit resources used, audio and resources are from appropriate sources—Creative Commons material or student can justify fair use	No citations of audio or inappropriate audio used or student unable to justify fair use
Legal and Ethical Guidelines	All course rules are followed consistently through the process	Course rules are followed for final production, but minor deviations occur during process	Repeated or significant violations of course rule throughout process

(continued)

Rubric for Unit 3: *The Metamorphosis:* **Audio Play Scripting** *(continued)*

	Related NETS·S	Related IRA/NCTE Standards	Related AASL Standards	Related TESOL Standards	Related WIDA Standards
Selection	1.a, 1.b, 3.b	2	1.1.6, 1.2.2, 1.2.3	1.1, 2.1, 2.3	1, 2—Reading
Transformation *(should be assessed in conference with students)*	2.a	3, 4	1.1.6, 1.2.2, 1.2.3, 1.4.2, 4.1.3, 4.1.8	1.3, 2.1, 2.2, 2.3	1, 2—Reading 1, 2—Writing 1—Speaking
Production	2.a, 6.a, 6.b, 6.d	3, 4	1.2.2, 1.2.3, 2.1.6, 3.1.3, 4.1.3, 4.1.8, 4.3.2	1.1, 2.3, 3.1	1—Reading 1—Speaking
Citations of Music and Sound Effects Resources	3.b, 5.a	4, 8	1.3.1, 1.3.3, 1.3.5, 3.1.6, 4.3.4		1—Speaking 1—Writing
Legal and Ethical Guidelines	5.a, 6.a		1.3.1, 1.3.3, 1.3.5, 3.1.6, 4.3.4		

Unit 4

Shakespearean
Audio Drama

Like the other fiction units, this activity capitalizes on the fact that in today's digital world people are becoming *simultaneous* consumers and creators of content. Copying and pasting, links, remixes, and mash-ups are increasingly popular ways to develop and communicate ideas in professional and social environments. Although this phenomenon can lead to problems such as plagiarism and copyright infringement, it also possible to ethically produce compelling and original works. This unit shows students and teachers how to appropriate and rework content in engaging and ethical ways.

This activity uses performance-based approaches to teaching Shakespeare as it focuses on engagement with Shakespeare's language. Students go *toward* Shakespeare's words and are scaffolded to take ownership, make decisions, and develop interpretations of the lines and scenes in performance—for real purposes and real audiences. Students learn how to give shape to their unique interpretations of Shakespeare's language and create original products using the content and material of others—effectively and legally.

Used under Creative Commons Attribution 2.0, image from www.flickr.com/photos/ryanrocketship/2724589320/

SUMMARY

Students create original audio dramas from scenes from Shakespeare's plays. They rehearse and record Shakespeare's language, add music and sound effects, and then shift, edit, and manipulate individual voices and sounds. Throughout the process they make interpretations and creative decisions as they take ownership of Shakespeare's work.

Specifically, for this unit students create an original audio drama of a scene from Shakespeare's *Julius Caesar*. The project uses text from the public domain and music and sound effects with Creative Commons licenses. Students enact all of the voices and add music and sound effects. You can have students work individually and create all of the voices, or you can modify the number of citizens in the scene based on the number of students in your groups and your time, resources, and goals. For example, you can have students work in groups of three and modify the cast to six citizens, with each student responsible for two voices (Shakespeare did these types of modifications all the time).

GRADE LEVELS

Grades 6–12

OBJECTIVES

- Distinguish different characters by changing vocal traits

- Create a scene from Shakespeare to entertain an audience

- Effectively and ethically integrate the material of others

TIME ALLOWANCE

3–7 days

RESOURCES

At least one computer with multitrack audio editing software and a microphone

If you are unfamiliar with performance-based approaches to teaching Shakespeare, you might find it worthwhile to look at the following two resources, which are good for actively engaging students in Shakespeare's language.

- *Shakespeare Set Free* (O'Brien, 1992)

- Cambridge School Shakespeare Series (Gibson)

Music and Sound Effects

You can have students search for sounds themselves or give them a group of sounds to choose from. I recommend using audio from sites that use Creative Commons licenses—The Creative Commons Mixter (www.ccmixter.org) for music and the Free Sounds Project (www.freesound.org) for sound effects. You might want to review the ideas from Chapter 3, Elements of Audio Drama, with your students.

A group of music and sound effect files for students to choose from is available at http://ccmixter.org/files/cs272/14753/. Here is a detailed list of the sounds in that zipped file:

Background Music

All of the following music is licensed with a Creative Commons Attribution 3.0 License (http://creativecommons.org/licenses/by/3.0/).

Fourmi 2 by Noelkay
    http://ccmixter.org/media/files/noelkay/12926

Natchoongi by Code
    http://ccmixter.org/media/files/Mixro/11243

You Asked for It (World is Different Mix) by DJ Blue
    http://ccmixter.org/media/files/DJBLUE/10756

Sound Effects

All of the following sound effects are licensed with a Creative Commons Sampling Plus 1.0 License (http://creativecommons.org/licenses/sampling+/1.0/).

Street sounds.mp3 from ERH
    http://freesound.iua.upf.edu/samplesViewSingle.php?id=42974

Turkish market.mp3 from Donalfonso
    http://freesound.iua.upf.edu/samplesViewSingle.php?id=43459

Cricket-2007-10-12.mp3 from Monterey2000
    http://freesound.iua.upf.edu/samplesViewSingle.php?id=43827

Procedures

I would suggest spending a class period on performing the scene so students can get an idea of its meaning in performance. Begin with a simple classroom reading of the scene. Next, divide the class into two or three groups of 8–12 students. Ask each group to cast, block, rehearse, and perform the scene. The entire class will see a variety of decisions and performances from the groups.

Provide students with Unit 4, Worksheets 1 and 2.

Now students can focus on adapting the scene for audio. Students should enact the parts, creating unique voices for each of the five characters with speaking parts. Next, students will add background music and sound effects. Finally, students will create a single mp3 file with all of these elements.

As with the other units, at the end of the scene students should briefly give credit to the source of their music and sound effect (see Unit 1: "I've Been Waiting for You" for more details).

Example

Here's an example with one student doing all of the characters:

http://podcourse.blogspot.com/2008/01/cinna-audio-play.html

Rubric for Unit 4: Shakespearean Audio Drama

	Exemplary	Satisfactory	Unacceptable
Dialogue	Consistent attempt to portray all characters uniquely with varying voices	Some but inconsistent attempt to portray each citizen and Cinna as a unique character with varying voices	No/little attempt to portray each citizen and Cinna as a unique character with varying voices
Music	Appropriate to scene and mixed to complement voices and action of the scene	Appropriate music during play, but sound levels occasionally interfere with voices	No music or inappropriate choice or use of music
Sound Effects	Sound effects add to the setting and plot of the scene	Appropriate sound effects but interfere with overall listening experience	No or inappropriate sound effects
Interpretation	Interpretation of scene is consistent and enhances the written dialogue	Interpretation of scene is generally consistent with written dialogue	Interpretation of scene is inconsistent with the written dialogue
Audio Quality	Music, sound effects, and dialogue are completely audible and complement each other. Audio file is appropriate length and size for the scene	Music, sound effects, and dialogue are generally audible, but some listening problems occur	Audio is inconsistent or significantly inaudible or unnecessarily large/long audio file
Citations of Music and Sound Effects Resources	Clear credit of resources in audio file from appropriate sources—listener can easily find source material, Creative Commons material, or student can justify fair use	Attempt to credit resources used, audio and resources are from appropriate sources—Creative Commons material or student can justify fair use	No citations of audio or inappropriate audio used or student unable to justify fair use
Legal and Ethical Guidelines	All course rules are followed consistently through the process	Course rules are followed for final production, but minor deviations occur during process	Repeated or significant violations of course rule throughout process

(continued)

Rubric for Unit 4: Shakespearean Audio Drama *(continued)*

	Related NETS•S	Related IRA/NCTE Standards	Related AASL Standards	Related TESOL Standards	Related WIDA Standards
Dialogue	1.a, 1.b, 2.a, 6.a, 6.b, 6.d	1, 2, 3, 4	4.1.3, 4.1.8	1.1, 3.1	1—Speaking 1—Reading
Music	1.a, 1.b, 2.a, 3.b, 6.a, 6.b, 6.d,	1, 2, 3	4.1.3, 4.1.8, 4.3.2		
Sound Effects	1.a, 1.b, 2.a, 3.b, 6.a, 6.b, 6.d,	1, 2, 3	4.1.3, 4.1.8, 4.3.2		
Interpretation	1.a, 1.b, 2.a, 6.a, 6.b, 6.d,	1, 2, 3, 4	4.1.3, 4.1.8	1.3, 2.2, 2.3, 3.1	1—Speaking 1—Reading
Audio Quality	1.a, 1.b, 2.a, 3.b, 6.a, 6.b, 6.d	1, 2, 3	4.1.3, 4.1.8		
Citations of Music and Sound Effects Resources	3.b, 5.a	4, 8	1.3.1, 1.3.3, 1.3.5, 3.1.6, 4.3.4		1—Speaking 1—Writing
Legal and Ethical Guidelines	5.a, 6.a		1.3.1, 1.3.3, 1.3.5, 3.1.6, 4.3.4		

Unit 5

Fanfiction

Fanfiction is the genre of writing in which students write original material based on existing stories, characters, and settings. It connects to the educational goals of intrinsically motivating students as well as participating in communities of practice and cultural creation (Jenkins, 2006; Shamburg, 2008).

SUMMARY

Students choose a fanfiction story based on a game, TV show, movie, comic book, or novel that they are fans of and create an original 3- to 6-minute audio show based on the chosen story. Students will write the script, enact the parts, and add music and sound effects. You might want to review the ideas from Chapter 3, Elements of Audio Drama with your students.

GRADE LEVELS

Grades 5–12

OBJECTIVES

- Articulate source material to a particular audience in an appropriate way
- Create an original story based on the stories of others
- Entertain a particular audience
- Use the medium of audio in an effective way
- Use the material of others ethically and effectively

TIME ALLOWANCE

5–14 days

RESOURCES

At least one computer with multitrack audio editing software and a microphone

Teachers may want to select stories from the following resources for students. It is difficult to find a fanfiction site without some mature content, though most will label mature stories with a rating or warning:

Lunaescence Archive
    www.lunaescence.com
    A moderated and rated source of fanfiction.

Fanfiction.net
>www.fanfiction.net
>A large collection of fanfiction with various topics, media, and genres.

Fanfiction sites at Squidoo
>www.squidoo.com/fanfictionsites/
>An annotated list of fanfiction sites with an overview of fanfiction.

Procedures

Discuss with students the following fanfiction story types (Shamburg, 2008):

Missing Scene. A scene that is not in the original story, but would make sense in the story. The missing scene would fill in some information that the original story left out. For example, what do the villains do in comic books when the story is focused on the superheroes?

Alternate Perspective. The story is told from the point of view of another character. For example, what would the Cinderella story be like if the stepmother told it?

Alternate Universe. A major character or event in a story is changed, and a "What If…" scenario ensues. For example, what if a radioactive ant bit Peter Parker?

Alternate Reality (Crossover). Characters from one story enter the world of another story. For example, what would happen if characters from one video game went to a different video game?

Sequel. The story that happens after the original story. For example, what does George do *after* the events in *Of Mice and Men*?

Prequel. The story before the original story. For example, what was Juliet doing before the events of the play?

Self Insert. The story is rewritten with an avatar (representation of the author). For example, what would a Harry Potter adventure be like if you were in the story?

Each student chooses source material that he or she is a fan of and writes three paragraphs explaining the plot of the source material and why it is interesting. Students then choose a fanfiction story based on the source material and submit a written transcript of their choice before recording. This transcript will be reviewed by the teacher for appropriateness. (The source material and chosen fanfiction story should have appropriate ratings—no material with R, Mature, Adult, or Explicit ratings.)

Students begin their audio show with a brief (15- to 30-second) explanation of the source material using the three paragraphs they have written. Students then create an audio fanfiction drama that employs music, sound effects, dialogue, and narration. Students cite the sources of their story and all music and sound effects used.

Example

Here is an example of audio fanfiction:

http://podcourse.blogspot.com/2008/11/fanfiction.html

Rubric for Unit 5: Fanfiction

	Exemplary	Satisfactory	Unacceptable
Background	Clearly and concisely explains the source material to a person unfamiliar with it enough so the listener can enjoy the original fanfiction	Explains the source material in a general way	Conveys a poor sense of context for fanfiction and source material
Original	New story is original and substantively extends the characters in the source material	New story is generally original, but does repeat themes or aspects of storylines of the original	New story lacks originality
Listener Interest	Events in fanfiction would interest both fans and those unfamiliar with the source material	Events in fanfiction would interest either fans *or* those unfamiliar with source material	Events in fanfiction would interest neither fans nor those unfamiliar with source material
Techniques	Narration, dialogue, music, and sound effects are employed effectively	Narration, dialogue, music, and sound effects are effective most of the time	Narration, dialogue, music, and sound effects do not work well together or are missing
Citations of Music and Sound Effects Resources	Clear credit of resources in audio file from appropriate sources—listener can easily find source material, Creative Commons material, or student can justify fair use	Attempt to credit resources used, audio and resources are from appropriate sources—Creative Commons material or student can justify fair use	No citations of audio or inappropriate audio used or student unable to justify fair use
Legal and Ethical Guidelines	All course rules are followed consistently through the process	Course rules are followed for final production, but minor deviations occur during process	Repeated or significant violations of course rule throughout process

(continued)

Rubric for Unit 5: Fanfiction *(continued)*

	Related NETS•S	Related IRA/NCTE Standards	Related AASL Standards	Related TESOL Standards	Related WIDA Standards
Background	3.b	1, 2, 11	1.1.6, 1.2.2, 4.1.5, 4.3.2	1.1, 2.2	1, 2— Speaking 1, 2— Writing
Original	1.a, 1.b	1, 2, 3, 4, 11	1.1.6, 3.1.3, 3.3.4, 4.1.3	1.3, 2.3	1, 2— Speaking 1, 2— Writing
Listener Interest	1.a, 1.b, 3.b	1, 2, 3, 4, 11	2.1.6, 3.1.3, 4.1.3	1.3, 2.3	1, 2— Speaking 1, 2— Writing
Techniques	1.a, 1.b, 3.b, 6.a, 6.b, 6.d	1, 2, 3, 4, 11	1.2.3, 2.1.6, 4.1.3, 4.3.2	3.1	
Citations of Music and Sound Effects Resources	3.b, 5.a	4, 8	1.3.1, 1.3.3, 1.3.5, 3.1.6, 4.3.4		
Legal and Ethical Guidelines	5.a, 6.a		1.3.1, 1.3.3, 1.3.5, 3.1.6, 4.3.4		

Unit 6

Character
Interview

The character interview is a way to invest students in the lives and experiences of fictional characters. It allows them the perspective and experience to expand beyond the information given in a story and make reasonable assumptions about the actions and motives of characters by bringing their experiences as well as historical context to bear. This type of analysis can be a launching point for contemporary approaches to historic and literary research.

SUMMARY

One student conducts an interview with a literary or historic character enacted by another student. In pairs, students develop, ask, answer, and record a three-question interview. This unit has worked successfully for novels such as *Of Mice and Men* and *To Kill a Mockingbird* and has been modified to work with younger students on books such as *The Cat in the Hat*.

GRADE LEVELS

Grades 3–12

OBJECTIVES

- Select facts and decisions from text
- Cite sources of information
- Develop questions and answers based on a careful reading of a text
- Enact an engaging and credible simulation of an interview
- Use the material of others effectively and ethically

TIME ALLOWANCE

1–2 weeks

RESOURCES

At least one computer with multitrack audio editing software and a microphone

Procedures

There are three general steps for this unit.

1. Research

2. Developing questions and answers

3. Conducting the interview

Here are the two guiding principles of the character interview:

1. The job of the interviewer is to put pressure on the interviewee to get information.

2. The job of the interviewee is to give his or her side of the story.

Assign students to pairs and have each pair choose a book or story with an interesting character to interview. Each pair should read through their chosen book or story and find the information below. They should quote directly from their book and cite the page number of the quote. For longer quotes, consider teaching students how to correctly use ellipses (...). Students should answer the following questions:

- How does the narrator describe the character?

- How does the character describe himself or herself?

- How do other characters describe the character?

- What are the three biggest actions and decisions of the character? These could have happened before or during the timeframe of the story.

Based on the answers to the questions above, students will develop their interview questions and answers. They should use the following phrases to introduce or transition their answers.

For interviewers:

- Why did you (important action or decision)?

- How do you (important action or decision)?

- But (another character) says you are...

- So you say (another character) is wrong when (he or she) says…

- Then why do many people think you are (narrator's description)…

For interviewees:

- Remember when I said (description by self)…

- Remember when I (narrative of actions)…

- Remember when I was described as a (other character's description)…

- I had reasons for saying that about myself…

- Most people would call me (author's description)…

- …Part of that is true, but it's more like…

- …That's not true, because I also…

- …I was like that at one point but now I'm…

Student should submit a written transcript of the interview for feedback from the teacher before recording.

Next, students record their interview, employing music, sound effects (if appropriate), and narration, and students cite their sources.

Example

http://podcourse.blogspot.com/interview/

Rubric for Unit 6: Character Interview

	Exemplary	Satisfactory	Unacceptable
Pre-Interview Decisions	3 major decisions listed	2 major decisions listed	0–1 major decision listed
Pre-Interview Resources	All/almost all of significant information with correct page numbers	Substantial amount of significant information with correct page numbers	Little or some significant information or no page numbers
Questions and Answers	Based on major decisions of character and uses material from story with logical and consistent explanations and evidence	Based on major decisions of character and uses material from story with reasonable explanations and evidence	Off topic or not important to the character or story
Audio	All of interview is clearly audible; appropriate dialects and intonations are used.	Most/all of interview is audible	Significant parts are inaudible
Citations of Music and Sound Effects Resources	Clear credit of resources in audio file from appropriate sources—listener can easily find source material, Creative Commons material, or student can justify fair use	Attempt to credit resources used, audio and resources are from appropriate sources—Creative Commons material or student can justify fair use	No citations of audio or inappropriate audio used or student unable to justify fair use
Legal and Ethical Guidelines	All course rules are followed consistently through the process	Course rules are followed for final production, but minor deviations occur during process	Repeated or significant violations of course rule throughout process

(continued)

Rubric for Unit 6: Character Interview *(continued)*

	Related NETS·S	Related IRA/NCTE Standards	Related AASL Standards	Related TESOL Standard	Related Social Studies Standards*	Related WIDA Standards
Pre-Interview Decisions		1, 2, 3	1.1.6, 1.2.2, 2.1.5, 3.2.3, 4.3.1	1.1, 1.3, 2.1, 2.2, 2.3	2, 3, 5	2—Reading 2—Speaking 2—Writing
Pre-Interview Resources		1, 2, 3	1.1.6, 1.2.2, 2.1.5, 3.2.3, 4.3.1	1.1, 1.3, 2.1, 2.2, 2.3	2, 3, 5	2—Reading 2—Writing
Questions and Answers	1.a, 1.b, 2.a, 3.b	1, 2, 3	1.1.6, 1.2.2, 2.1.5, 3.2.3, 4.3.1	1.1, 1.3, 2.2, 2.3	2, 3, 5	2—Reading 2—Writing
Audio	1.a, 1.b, 2.a, 3.b, 6.a, 6.b, 6.d	1, 2, 3, 4	3.1.3, 3.2.3, 4.1.3, 4.1.8	1.1, 2.2, 3.1		1—Speaking 1—Reading 2—Writing
Citations of Music and Sound Effects Resources	3.b, 5.a	4, 8	1.3.1, 1.3.3, 1.3.5, 3.1.6, 4.3.4			1—Speaking 1—Writing
Legal and Ethical Guidelines	5.a, 6.a		1.3.1, 1.3.3, 1.3.5, 3.1.6, 4.3.4			

Applicable if focus is on historical figure.

Unit 7

Media Review

For this project students will review some form of media—a book, a TV show, an episode of a TV series, a video game, a song, or an album. This project emphasizes the importance of audience and purpose for student podcasters. It also capitalizes on their current interests. A great service we can do as educators is to teach students that their interests, lives, and experiences have value—to us, to them, and to the outside world. Validating the worth and dignity of individuals has moral value, but it also makes sense from a purely educational perspective. It is educationally valuable because student interests do not occur in a vacuum. There are inevitable connections to larger trends and bigger ideas that students will discover—will *want* to discover—as they explore and explain their own interests.

Teaching students to expand and connect with their interests is socially and economically important as well. Because like-minded people can connect across space in communities and business in financial, social, and political activities, it is crucial that people hone the self-management skills of intrinsic motivation.

The process of producing for real purposes and real audiences—the other focus of this unit—is a crucial learning tool as well. First of all, this prepares students for the types of activities that they will do outside of school. Second, the authenticity of a "real purpose and real audience" acts as the organizing feature of the content and style. Consider topics such as "Describe Hamlet's Problem" or "Explain the Causes of the Civil War," topics that represent a more traditional approach to education. Many students approach topics such as these with some confusion as to the type of background information to include or the amount of exposition to give because the audience—the teacher—is perceived as having mastery over the topic. The student perceives an essay such as this as a foreign task because it lacks a meaningful context. However, when the student has to actually reflect and consider the background knowledge and interests of an intended audience—when these estimations are real and have value—the organization and style of the work can be done purposefully.

SUMMARY

Students record an audio review some form of media—a book, a TV show, an episode of a TV series, a video game, a song, or an album—taking into account their own interests and their intended audience.

GRADE LEVELS

Grades 5–12

OBJECTIVES

- Thoughtfully address selected audience's expectations, interests, and prior knowledge

- Review main ideas of a piece of media

- Convey opinion with evidence

- Use the material of others effectively and ethically

TIME ALLOWANCE

3–5 days

RESOURCES

At least one computer with multitrack audio editing software and a microphone

Procedures

Introduce students to the purpose of media reviews: to inform, warn, or persuade others. This can be done as a class discussion.

Then students select content to review and choose their intended audience (Unit 7, Worksheet 1). Unit 7, Worksheet 2 can be used to begin this brainstorming and organization as students write their reviews for their intended audiences. Teachers should review students' work. (The media chosen for review should not have an R, Mature, or Adult rating.)

Once students have an approved draft in written form, they can record their voices. Here you should focus their attention on an engaging speaking style. The review should be between 1 and 3 minutes and should follow the Review Template (see Unit 7, Worksheet 2).

Consider allowing students to include a clip of the reviewed media after discussing with them fair use guidelines (see Appendix A).

Examples

The link below has four examples of this project:

http://podcourse.blogspot.com/2007/03/media-reviews-this-episode-shares-some.html

Rubric for Unit 7: Media Review

	Exemplary	Satisfactory	Unacceptable
Audience	Obvious effort to make review clear and interesting for audience, and clear, standard English is used	Content and style generally appropriate for audience, and clear, standard English is used	Little/no consideration for audience and/or nonstandard English used
Introduction	Interests listeners in the podcast	Some attempt to interest listeners	Little/no attempt to interest listeners
Identify Topic	Clearly identifies subject of review early in podcast	Identifies subject of review early in podcast	Subject of review is unclear
Background	Effective background, context, history, and related information	Discussion of background, context, history, and related information	No/little background, context, history, or related information
Opinion	Opinion with some detailed reasoning	Some version of an opinion with reason	No or unclear opinion
Support	Concise and persuasive reasons and explanations	Some/several supporting reasons and explanations	No supporting reasons or explanations
Speaking Style	Engaging and lively	Clear with few distractions	Dull/monotone/ distractingly unclear
Recommendation	Recommendation that matches rest of the review and appropriate for audience	Recommendation generally supported by rest of review	No recommendation or unsupported by rest of review
Legal and Ethical Guidelines	All course rules are followed consistently through the process	Course rules are followed for final production, but minor deviations occur during process	Repeated or significant violations of course rule throughout process

(continued)

Rubric for Unit 7: Media Review *(continued)*

	Related NETS•S	Related IRA/NCTE Standards	Related AASL Standards	Related TESOL Standards	Related WIDA Standards
Audience	1.b, 4.a, 6.a, 6.d	2, 4, 5, 6	2.1.1, 2.1.2, 2.3.1, 4.1.3	1.2, 1.3, 2.2, 3.3	1—Speaking 1—Writing
Introduction	1.b, 4.a, 6.a, 6.d	2, 6		1.2, 1.3, 2.2, 3.3	1—Speaking 1—Writing
Identify Topic	1.b, 6.a, 6.d	1, 2, 6	1.2.2	1.2, 1.3, 2.2, 3.3	1—Speaking 1—Writing
Background	1.b, 6.a, 6.d	2, 6	1.1.4, 1.2.1	1.2, 1.3, 2.2, 3.3	1—Speaking 1—Writing
Opinion	1.a, 1.b, 6.a, 6.d	2, 6	1.1.2	1.2, 1.3, 2.2, 3.3	1—Speaking 1—Writing
Support	1.b, 6.a, 6.d	2, 6		1.2, 1.3, 2.2, 3.3	1—Speaking 1—Writing
Speaking Style	1.b, 6.a, 6.d	2, 4, 6		1.2, 1.3, 2.2, 3.3	1—Speaking 1—Writing
Recommendation	1.b, 6.a, 6.d	2, 6	2.3.1	1.2, 1.3, 2.2, 3.3	1—Speaking 1—Writing
Legal and Ethical Guidelines	5.a, 6.a		1.3.1, 1.3.3, 1.3.5, 3.1.6, 4.3.4		

Unit 8

Remixing
Primary Sources

In this project students vocally enact excerpts from letters, journals, speeches, and interviews. This idea borrows heavily from such works as Studs Terkel's *American Dreams: Lost and Found* and Anna Deavere Smith's *Fires in the Mirror*. Both of these works take interviews from American citizens and turn them into poignant literary and performance pieces. This project takes that authentic and powerful idea and fundamentally recasts it with digital media.

SUMMARY

Students are given a set of source types—historically significant sources (e.g., the Gettysburg Address, Kennedy's Inaugural Address), personal history (e.g., letters, diary entries), and/or social history (cookbooks, radio broadcasts) and must integrate them in a single audio performance. They can work from multiple media—for example, reading texts themselves and using actual historical broadcasts—as well as integrate ambient music. The idea is to connect larger trends and events in history with the personal and social experiences of everyday people.

GRADE LEVELS

Grades 5–8

OBJECTIVES

- Identify diverse primary sources with similar themes
- Clearly and appropriately read primary sources
- Mix materially purposefully and creatively
- Use the material of others effectively and ethically

TIME ALLOWANCE

3 days to 2 weeks

RESOURCES

At least one computer with multitrack audio editing software and a microphone

History Websites

You might want to begin by giving students a list of suggested sources, particularly if you are studying a particular period of history. Two sites I recommend are American Memory from the Library of Congress (http://memory.loc.gov) and the Internet Archive (www.archive.org). The breadth and depth of both sources are amazing and worth a browse by any teacher or student. You should also stay open to student suggestions.

American Memory project from the Library of Congress
http://memory.loc.gov/ammem/
This site contains interviews, recordings, videos, and maps that
document the American experience. You can get digital material
such as songs from Depression-era railroad gangs to videos of Teddy
Roosevelt's Rough Riders in Cuba.

Internet Archive
www.archive.org
The Internet Archive is a nonprofit initiative that collects and
disseminates cultural, social, and historical material digitally. You
will find a variety of fascinating material, from public service
announcements from the 1950s to recordings of Grateful Dead
concerts.

Music

You might also want to let the students to add ambient music. I have a
collection of ambient tracks here:

> http://ccmixter.org/files/cs272/15836/

Procedures

As a model or warm-up activity, you can have students work in pairs to remix
two of these three primary sources:

- Lou Gehrig's farewell speech in which he calls himself "The luckiest
  man on the face of this earth" (see next page)

- Excerpts from *The Spalding Base Ball Guide,* 1939
  (http://memory.loc.gov/ammem/collections/spalding/) (see next page)

- The radio broadcast from the 1936 World Series in which Lou Gehrig
  hits a home run in the second inning (www.archive.org/details/
  361003WorldSeriesGiantsVsYankees) from the Internet Archive

Lou Gehrig's farewell speech, July 4, 1939:

Fans, for the past two weeks you have been reading about the bad break I got. Yet today I consider myself the luckiest man on the face of this earth. I have been in ballparks for seventeen years and have never received anything but kindness and encouragement from you fans.

Look at these grand men. Which of you wouldn't consider it the highlight of his career just to associate with them for even one day? Sure, I'm lucky. Who wouldn't consider it an honor to have known Jacob Ruppert? Also, the builder of baseball's greatest empire, Ed Barrow? To have spent six years with that wonderful little fellow, Miller Huggins? Then to have spent the next nine years with that outstanding leader, that smart student of psychology, the best manager in baseball today, Joe McCarthy? Sure, I'm lucky.

When the New York Giants, a team you would give your right arm to beat, and vice versa, sends you a gift—that's something. When everybody down to the groundskeepers and those boys in white coats remember you with trophies—that's something. When you have a wonderful mother-in-law who takes sides with you in squabbles with her own daughter—that's something. When you have a father and a mother who work all their lives so you can have an education and build your body—it's a blessing. When you have a wife who has been a tower of strength and shown more courage than you dreamed existed—that's the finest I know.

So I close in saying that I may have had a tough break, but I have an awful lot to live for.

Excerpts from "Official Playing Rules of American Ball Clubs" from *The Spalding Base Ball Guide*, 1939:

Rule 2. Diamond or Infield…. A simple method of laying out a ball field with a piece of cord is as follows: First—Get a piece of rope or cord, with no stretch in it. Second—Measure off the following distances and make a knot at each distance: 60 feet 6 inches—90 feet—127 feet 3 inches—180 feet. Third—Decide upon the location of home plate (north and south is preferable, to avoid the sun in the fielders' eyes).

Rule 19. Players in uniform shall not be permitted to occupy seats or to mingle with spectators.

Rule 23. It is a regulation game if it be called by the umpire on account of darkness, rain, fire, panic, or for other causes that puts players in peril.

Rule 53. Umpires and their duties. In order to define their respective duties, the umpire judging balls and strikes shall be designated "Umpire in Chief." The umpire judging base decisions, the "Field Umpire."

Before starting on the remix project, you should discuss with the students the artistic and emotional effects of pairing the two chosen sources. How do the works relate to each other? How do they contrast with each other? What effect are students looking to create with their remix that is not present in the individual works?

In pairs, students should work on a transcript showing how they will remix their primary sources, what music or sound effects they intend to use, and how they will cite their sources. You will review these transcripts before students record.

When students choose their own topics, you should allow them to work from their interests. In addition to sports, students can find primary source material related to topics such as fashion, music, and local history.

Example

Here is an example that uses the material from the model lesson above:

http://podcourse.blogspot.com/primary-source.htm

Rubric for Unit 8: Remixing Primary Sources

	Exemplary	Satisfactory	Unacceptable
Choice of Two Sources— Different, Significant	Sources represent different points of view but with similar themes	Sources represent different topics, but from same time period or subject	Little or superficial connection between two sources
Readings— Appropriate and Clear	Readings are clear and distinct with effective tones and speed	Readings are clear and appropriate for topic	Readings are unclear or inappropriate for topic
Mixing— Purposeful	Mix creates a unique experience beyond the individual sources and tracks	Mix highlights the importance of each source	Mix does not effectively present both primary sources
Citations of Music and Sound Effects Resources	Clear credit of resources in audio file from appropriate sources—listener can easily find source material, Creative Commons material, or student can justify fair use	Attempt to credit resources used, audio and resources are from appropriate sources— Creative Commons material or student can justify fair use	No citations of audio or inappropriate audio used or student unable to justify fair use
Legal and Ethical Guidelines	All course rules are followed consistently through the process	Course rules are followed for final production, but minor deviations occur during process	Repeated or significant violations of course rule throughout process

(continued)

Rubric for Unit 8: Remixing Primary Sources (continued)

	Related NETS•S	Related IRA/NCTE Standards	Related AASL Standards	Related TESOL Standard	Related Social Studies Standards*	Related WIDA Standards
Choice of Two Sources—Different, Significant	3.b	1, 2, 8	1.1.5, 1.1.6, 1.2.2, 1.2.3		2, 3, 4	2—Reading 5—Reading
Readings—Appropriate and Clear		1, 2, 3, 4		1.3, 2.2, 3.1	2, 3, 4	2, 5—Speaking 2, 5—Reading
Mixing—Purposeful	1.a, 1.b, 3.b, 6.a, 6.d	6, 8	1.2.3, 2.1.1, 4.1.8	2.2, 3.3	2, 3, 4	
Citations of Music and Sound Effects Resources	3.b, 5.a	4, 8	1.3.1, 1.3.3, 1.3.5, 3.1.6, 4.3.4			1—Speaking 1—Writing
Legal and Ethical Guidelines	5.a, 6.a		1.3.1, 1.3.3, 1.3.5, 3.1.6, 4.3.4			

Applicable if focus is on historical figure.

Unit 9

Memoir

For this project students will write and record a memoir. Our working definition of a memoir is that it is a story from the writer's life based on his or her memories. This project incorporates two powerful ideas. Students will focus on the power of the human voice—its cadences, inflection, speed, and silences—to emotionally affect an audience. Additionally, this unit is based on developmental approaches to writing, with the belief that students are more concerned and invested in their writing when it connects to their lives.

The subject of each memoir can be funny, sad, exciting, or unique. It should be a story that interests the student as well as an audience. It could be an event that happened once, or it could be an event that happens repeatedly, such as a family tradition.

You should emphasize that any event can be boring or interesting—it all depends on how it is told, what order the events are put in, and what details the teller decides to include. Remind the students that they are inviting listeners to share an experience.

SUMMARY

Each student writes a memoir, relating an event in three to four pages and considering how to make it interesting and engaging for their audience. Then, each student records his or her memoir in a way that will hold the interest of listeners. Vocal performance, music, and sound effects all contribute to the oral memoir.

GRADE LEVELS

Grades 5–12

OBJECTIVES

- Create an engaging story for a targeted audience
- Organize ideas for an engaging story
- Develop main story with supporting details
- Write story in clear and effective style
- Use techniques of spoken language effectively

TIME ALLOWANCE

4–8 days

RESOURCES

At least one computer with multitrack audio editing software and a microphone

Procedures

Directions for the students as they write:

- Your memoir should be from 3 to 4 pages long (2 to 4 minutes when spoken).

- There should be no information that would greatly embarrass other people (or yourself).

- Your story should have a beginning where you set the story or catch the listener's attention.

- Your story should have an end—some conclusion, moral, lesson, punch line—something that tells a listener that it is over.

- You will add music to set a mood and to help with transitions, especially if your story takes place over a long period of time.

- Consider whether the use of sound effects would be appropriate and engaging.

Here are some guiding questions that you should use to scaffold the students:

- How does this memoir begin?

- What makes this interesting?

- How does it end?

Here are some subjects from past memoir projects:

- My first day in the United States

- The day my bike got stolen

- The time my friends and I found a strange chemical in an empty lot

- Sunday dinner at my grandmother's house

- Playing football in the dark during summer

The subject can be almost anything! You should approve all topics and review the transcripts of the memoirs before students begin recording.

Examples

Here are several examples of the memoir project:
http://podcourse.blogspot.com/2007/04/memoir-project-part-1.html

Here's an example in which I remixed the student's work with my feedback:
http://podcourse.blogspot.com/2008/02/more-on-memoirs.html

Rubric for Unit 9: Memoir

	Exemplary	Satisfactory	Unacceptable
Event Presented in an Interesting Way	Obvious care to engage, inform, and entertain audience	Some care to engage, inform, and entertain audience	Little/no care to engage, inform, and entertain audience
Beginning	Interesting hook or concise and interesting setup for the story	Somewhat interesting beginning	No interesting hook or lack of background information to set up listener for story
Details	Details proceed in an interesting way, intended to inform and entertain the audience	Quality and quantity of details generally appropriate	Details of the story proceed in an uninteresting way, missing, or excessive
End	Effective ending, conclusion, punch line, or moral	Ending is conclusive but lacks compelling power	No conclusion, resolution, punch line, or moral
Narration/ Vocals	Effective use of emotional changes in voice	Generally effective use of voice throughout most of the recording	Few/no or ineffective changes in tone or voice
Music	Appropriate use of music	Music used appropriately through most of the recording	Inappropriate/lack of music in story
Citations of Music and Sound Effects Resources	Clear credit of resources in audio file from appropriate sources—listener can easily find source material, Creative Commons material, or student can justify fair use	Attempt to credit resources used, audio and resources are from appropriate sources—Creative Commons material or student can justify fair use	No citations of audio or inappropriate audio used or student unable to justify fair use
Legal and Ethical Guidelines	All course rules are followed consistently through the process	Course rules are followed for final production, minor deviations occur during process	Repeated or significant violations of course rule throughout process

(continued)

Rubric for Unit 9: Memoir *(continued)*

	Related NETS·S	Related IRA/NCTE Standards	Related AASL Standards	Related TESOL Standards	Related WIDA Standards
Event Presented in an Interesting Way	1.a, 1.b, 6a, 6d	4, 6	1.1.5, 1.1.8, 1.2.2, 4.1.8	1.2, 1.3, 2.2, 3.3	1, 2— Writing 1, 2— Speaking
Beginning		4, 6	1.1.5, 1.1.8, 1.2.2, 4.1.8	1.2, 1.3, 2.2, 3.3	1, 2— Writing 1, 2— Speaking
Details	1.a, 1.b, 6a, 6d	4, 6	1.1.5, 1.1.8, 1.2.2, 4.1.8	1.2, 1.3, 2.2, 3.3	1, 2— Writing 1, 2— Speaking
End	1.a, 1.b, 6a, 6d	4, 6	1.1.5, 1.1.8, 1.2.2, 4.1.8	1.2, 1.3, 2.2, 3.3	1, 2— Writing 1, 2— Speaking
Narration/ Vocals	1.a, 1.b, 6a, 6d	4, 6	1.1.5, 1.1.8, 1.2.2, 4.1.8	1.2, 1.3, 2.2, 3.3	1, 2— Writing 1, 2— Speaking
Music	1.a, 1.b, 6a, 6d		1.1.5, 1.1.8, 1.2.2, 4.1.8, 4.3.2		
Citations of Music and Sound Effects Resources	3.b, 5.a	4, 8	1.3.1, 1.3.3, 1.3.5, 3.1.6, 4.3.4		1—Speaking 1—Writing
Legal and Ethical Guidelines	5.a, 6.a		1.3.1, 1.3.3, 1.3.5, 3.1.6, 4.3.4		

Unit 10

Poetry Walk
Remix

The purpose of this project is to make an audio mix that will help people enjoy their environment as they walk or run. It is based on DJ Steveboy's Podrunner (www.djsteveboy.com/mixes.html), a podcast begun in February 2006 that is one of the most downloaded music podcasts on iTunes. Podrunner provides musical mixes at different tempos for various aerobic and cardio activities.

This unit goes to the heart of poetry appreciation—students are forced to slow down their reading, reflect on lines of poetry, and read and reread them to themselves and aloud. It presents longer, more complex poems in developmentally appropriate ways by allowing students to focus on individual lines under their own volition. This unit is also based on the Romantic poets' belief in the transformative powers of the poetic imagination to enliven experience.

Used by permission of Podrunner, LLC (www.podrunner.com)

SUMMARY

Students create a poetry remix to be listened to on a portable device (iPod or mp3 player) as a person walks or runs through a natural setting (woods or park) or an urban setting (city street). The students' remixes will contain music and lines from poetry. They can use their own voices or you can have students share raw clips of recited poetry and they can remix each other's voices in their final productions.

GRADE LEVELS

Grades 4–12

OBJECTIVES

- Select lines of poetry that convey a meaning that is significant to the theme of the remix
- Speak lines of poetry with appropriate tones and effect
- Integrate poetry and music appropriately for a setting
- Create a mix to engage a person in their nature or city walk
- Use the material of others effectively and ethically

TIME ALLOWANCE

3–6 days

RESOURCES

At least one computer with multitrack audio editing software and a microphone

Poetry

Below I have given the poetry that I use with my students. Feel free to use this or to select your own material.

"I Am the People, the Mob" by Carl Sandburg (urban setting)
   http://carl-sandburg.com/i_am_the_people_the_mob.htm

"Chicago" by Carl Sandburg (urban setting)
   http://carl-sandburg.com/chicago.htm

"Evangeline" by Henry Wadsworth Longfellow (natural setting)
   www.theotherpages.org/poems/books/longfellow/evangeline00.html

"Lines Written a Few Miles Above Tintern Abbey" by William Wordsworth (natural setting)
   www.online-literature.com/wordsworth/lyrical-ballads-1798/23/

"A Child Said, What Is the Grass?" by Walt Whitman (natural setting)
   www.poets.org/viewmedia.php/prmMID/15816/

"Song of Myself" by Walt Whitman (natural or urban setting)
   http://etext.virginia.edu/etcbin/toccer-new2?id=Whi91LG.
   sgm&images=images/modeng&data=/texts/english/modeng/
   parsed&tag=public&part=26&division=div2

Selected Lines of Poetry

Below are some lines that can be selected from the poems. They are used in the audio mixes in the examples.

Natural Setting

"The smallest sprouts show there is really no death" ("A Child Said, What Is the Grass?" by Walt Whitman)

"Have you reckon'd a thousand acres much? have you reckon'd the earth much?" ("Leaves of Grass" by Walt Whitman)

"You shall possess the good of the earth and sun, (there are millions of suns left)" ("Leaves of Grass" by Walt Whitman)

"This is the forest primeval. The murmuring pines and the hemlocks, Bearded with moss" ("Evangeline" by Henry Wadsworth Longfellow)

"I bounded o'er the mountains, by the sides, Of the deep rivers, and the lonely streams" ("Lines Written a Few Miles Above Tintern Abbey" by William Wordsworth)

Urban Setting

"I am the workingman, the inventor, the maker of the world's food and clothes." ("I Am the People, the Mob" by Carl Sandburg)

"Come and show me another city with lifted head singing so proud to be alive and coarse and strong and cunning ... Bragging and laughing that under his wrist is the pulse. and under his ribs the heart of the people." ("Chicago" by Carl Sandburg)

"This is the city and I am one of the citizens. Whatever interests the rest interests me, politics, wars, markets, newspapers, schools." ("Leaves of Grass" by Walt Whitman)

Music

Here is a collection of music clips that were used in the two examples presented in the project. Feel free to use these or look for your own.

http://ccmixter.org/files/cs272/15836

Procedures

This project has two parts. The first part consists of selecting, recording, and sharing lines of poetry. Depending on their level, you can give students full poems or selected lines, or you can have them select poems themselves. Students should study their selected poetry for meaning and should practice reading it in engaging ways. Students might choose to have other students read their poetry in order to have more than one voice in their remix. Students can also choose appropriate music and consider adding sound effects.

During the second part students create their remixes. Their chosen poetry should enhance the setting they have chosen, their reading of the poetry should be interesting and engaging, and the music and sound effects they select should complement the poetry. Their remixes should each run four to five minutes. Students should cite the sources of their chosen poetry, music, and sound effects.

Examples

Here are examples of both remixes: natural setting and urban setting.

Natural: http://podcourse.blogspot.com/2009/04/poetry-walk-remix-nature.html

Urban: http://podcourse.blogspot.com/2008/05/poetry-walk-remix-city.html

Rubric for Unit 10: Poetry Walk Remix

	Exemplary	Satisfactory	Unacceptable
Selection of Lines	Lines convey individual and complete ideas; capture the appropriate setting: urban or nature	Lines generally convey interesting and complete ideas; generally capture setting	Lines are random or inappropriate; capture fractured or incomplete ideas
Appropriate and Various Voices/Effects	Varied, interesting, and engaging speech and effects	Varied speech and effects	Monotonous speech and effects; inaudible
Connection among Music, Poetry, and Setting	Strong connection among music, poetry, and setting	Connection among music, poetry, and setting	Little/no connection among music, poetry, and setting
Quality of Mixing	All elements of voice, music, and effects create a single, seamless effect	Elements of voice, music, and effects generally create single effect with some mistakes and disruptions	Voice, music, and effects disconnected and/or distracting
Citations of Music and Sound Effects Resources	Clear credit of resources in audio file from appropriate sources—listener can easily find source material, Creative Commons material, or student can justify fair use	Attempt to credit resources used, audio and resources are from appropriate sources—Creative Commons material or student can justify fair use	No citations of audio or inappropriate audio used or student unable to justify fair use
Legal and Ethical Guidelines	All course rules are followed consistently through the process	Course rules are followed for final production, but minor deviations occur during process	Repeated or significant violations of course rule throughout process

(continued)

Rubric for Unit 10: Poetry Walk Remix *(continued)*

	Related NETS·S	Related IRA/NCTE Standards	Related AASL Standards	Related TESOL Standard	Related Social Studies Standards	Related WIDA Standards
Selection of Lines		1, 2, 3	1.1.6, 1.2.2, 4.1.2	2.2, 2.3	1, 2, 3	2—Reading
Appropriate and Various Voices/Effects		3, 4, 6		2.2, 2.3, 3.1		2—Speaking
Connection among Music, Poetry, and Setting		3	1.1.2, 3.3.1, 4.1.2		1, 2, 3	
Quality of Mixing	1.a, 1.b, 3.b, 6.a, 6.b, 6.d	3, 6	1.2.3, 2.2.4, 3.3.1			
Citations of Music and Sound Effects Resources	3.b, 5.a	4, 8	1.3.1, 1.3.3, 1.3.5, 3.1.6, 4.3.4			1—Speaking 1—Writing
Legal and Ethical Guidelines	5.a, 6.a		1.3.1, 1.3.3, 1.3.5, 3.1.6, 4.3.4			

Unit 11

Audio Tour

This project was inspired by the Art Mobs Project (http://mod.blogs.com/art_mobs/), an initiative that had students create original and engaging audio tours of museums in New York City. The podcasts of the audio tours were then available for download and use during the physical tour of the museum. It was a great opportunity to capitalize on the gap between ubiquitous audio tours of museums, which could seem distant and disconnected to students, and the students' desire and ability to impress meaning on places that were important to them. It was also an innovative and increasingly popular use of podcasting.

SUMMARY

Students choose a public place that has meaning to them and create an audio tour for it. They combine their personal interests and experiences with historical information and interviews with other people who had experience with or insight into the place. Past choices have included a restaurant that a student's family went to every week in Chinatown, a student's church that was converted from an old movie palace, and a local park where a student would spend time with his brother.

GRADE LEVELS

Grades 6–12

OBJECTIVES

- Select an appropriate location for tour that would interest a particular audience

- Describe main features and supporting details to engage a listener

- Research appropriate background for tour

- Synthesize interview with relevant person on tour site

TIME ALLOWANCE

5–8 days

RESOURCES

At least one computer with multitrack audio editing software and a microphone

Procedures

Below are the directions for the students.

1. Describe the location (directions are optional).

2. Tell about the background of the place (information such as its importance to the rest of the town, its history, its origin). Cite the sources of this information. Who told you or where did you find this information? Did it come from a person, website, or book?

3. Describe the place as you walk through or someone else drives you through (three to five interesting areas within it with descriptions, and reasons why these areas are interesting).

4. Provide one or more quotes from at least one other person about this place or part of the place. You can record their voice or write down and repeat their quotes, but you must get their permission first.

5. What else would you like to add to make the tour useful and interesting? You should add music, sound effects, ambient sounds from the actual place, and/or interviews with other people in your final tour. You can present the required information in whatever order you think makes sense, though I would strongly suggest beginning with the location.

6. Submit a transcript of your podcast before recording. We will review this in conference.

7. Record and mix your podcast.

8. Consider asking someone to listen to your audio tour as they tour the location and using their feedback to improve your audio tour.

Example

http://podcourse.blogspot.com/2008/11/audio-tour.html

Rubric for Unit 11: Audio Tour

	Exemplary	Satisfactory	Unacceptable
Choice of Location	Public place that is made interesting to listener	Public place that a listener can tour	Private or restricted area
Description	Includes main features, supporting details that are interesting to audience; easy to follow while listening at location; personal connection of the narrator to the place is evident	Includes main features but missing appropriate supporting detail or occasionally difficult to follow	Lacking main features, supporting details or uninteresting; difficult to follow when listening at location; little or no description of the personal connection or interest in the place
Background	Sufficient and cited background information on history or context of place	Some historic detail, properly cited	Little or no context or history of location; poor or no citations of background information
Interview	Interview (recorded or quoted by narrator) significantly enriches tour experience	Interview present and generally supporting tour	Lacking effective or appropriate interview
Music/Effects	Appropriate and effective use of ambient sounds enhances tour	Some use of music and ambient sounds—does not distract from tour	Little or no appropriate music or sounds (effects or ambient noises)
Narration/Tone	Clear, engaging, and appropriate tone. Humorous and/or interesting	Generally clear speaking tone	Unclear, inappropriate, or unengaging tone
Citations of Music and Sound Effects Resources	Clear credit of resources in audio file from appropriate sources—listener can easily find source material, Creative Commons material, or student can justify fair use	Attempt to credit resources used, audio and resources are from appropriate sources—Creative Commons material or student can justify fair use	No citations of audio or inappropriate audio used or student unable to justify fair use
Legal and Ethical Guidelines	All course rules are followed consistently through the process	Course rules are followed for final production, minor deviations occur during process	Repeated or significant violations of course rule throughout process

(continued)

Rubric for Unit 11: Audio Tour *(continued)*

	Related NETS·S	Related IRA/NCTE Standards	Related AASL Standards	Related TESOL Standard	Related Social Studies Standards	Related WIDA Standards
Choice of Location	1.a		1.1.2, 2.3.1, 4.4.1		2, 3	
Description	1.b	4, 5	1.1.2, 3.1.3	1.3, 2.2, 3.1	2, 3	1, 2—Speaking 1, 2—Writing
Background		4, 5, 7	1.1.2, 1.1.3, 1.1.4, 1.1.6	2.2	2, 3	2, 5—Speaking 2, 5—Writing
Interview	2.a	4, 5, 7	1.1.2, 1.1.3, 1.1.4, 1.1.6, 3.3.2	1.1	2, 3	1, 2—Speaking 1, 2—Writing
Music/Effects	1.b		2.1.6			
Narration/Tone		4				
Citations of Music and Sound Effects Resources	3.b, 5.a	4, 8	1.3.1, 1.3.3, 1.3.5, 3.1.6, 4.3.4			1—Speaking 1—Writing
Legal and Ethical Guidelines	5.a, 6.a		1.3.1, 1.3.3, 1.3.5, 3.1.6, 4.3.4			

Unit 12

By Lisa Bucciarelli

Foreign Language
Podcasting

Podcasting is an ideal way to develop speaking skills, chronicle growth, and reduce the phobias associated with speaking in a foreign language. Students gain a greater sense of control over their speaking and the ability to immediately hear their own voices.

This activity can be used in a variety of ways. Students can create their own podcasts and submit them to the teacher, or students can exchange the files and then use the material in the podcasts as starting points for conversational skills in class.

This unit can also be adapted as an assessment tool at the end of a unit. This is an example of an alternative assessment for oral exams that can be adapted for all languages from levels I to V.

SUMMARY

This unit provides students with opportunities to use the target language frequently and develop confidence in their speaking skills. Students create podcasts in the target language by responding to thematic questions with short answers (60–90 seconds).

GRADE LEVELS

Grades 6–12

OBJECTIVES

- To incorporate key vocabulary
- To effectively organize the main idea and present details
- To effectively communicate in the target language with minimal errors
- To create an audio file and post it to an assigned space

TIME ALLOWANCE

1–3 days

RESOURCES

At least one computer with multitrack audio editing software and a microphone

Suggested themes for 60-second podcasts are:

- Who are you? (Based on appropriate vocabulary)
- What not to wear according to _____.
- Your dream house: what does it have?
- Where do you live and go to school?

- Describe your family.

- Describe your personal interests and hobbies.

- Why are you a good candidate for studying abroad?

- Describe a cultural event in _____.

- Describe the perfect restaurant.

Procedures

1. Choose a topic based on the suggested themes.

2. Students can write a rough draft of their answers and then record their podcasts. Or, depending on their proficiency, the recordings could be spontaneous.

3. Listen to the podcasts in class.

4. Solicit peer feedback. Allow students a chance to respond to their class-mates' work. This ensures that students are listening to their peers.

Example

http://drbpodcasts.wetpaint.com

This link contains the following topics:

- Who am I?

- My family

- What not to wear according to _____

- The perfect restaurant, an interview

Rubric for Unit 12: Foreign Language Podcasting

	4 Exemplary	3 Very Good	2 Satisfactory	1 Unacceptable
Vocabulary	Precise and effective word choice, impressive and broad use of vocabulary; sophisticated for level	Very few erroneous words, good use of words studied; impressive vocabulary or level	Adequate word choice, some erroneous words but meaning is conveyed; satisfactory for level	Inadequate for level, invented words, meaning is not properly conveyed; not acceptable for level
Organization	Effectively organized, main idea presented and details connect logically; excellent control of theme	Main idea presented, evidence of ideas connected to theme, details presented	Main idea presented, but not well connected to theme; details do not connect to main idea	Lacks main idea and logical sequence of details and/or lacks presentation theme
Convention of Language	No errors; effective and fluid	Very few errors; effective and fluid	Many errors, but comprehensible	Systemic errors; incomprehensible
Audio Quality	Audible and easy to hear	Audible with some distractions	Poor sound quality	Inaudible

(continued)

Rubric for Unit 12: Foreign Language Podcasting *(continued)*

	Related NETS•S	Related AASL Standards	Related Social Studies Standards	Related ACTFL Standards
Vocabulary	1.a, 1.b, 2.a, 2.b, 2.d,	2.16, 3.12, 3.13, 4.15		1.2, 1.3
Organization	1.b, 6.a, 6.d	2.16, 3.12, 3.13, 4.15	1, 2, 3, 4	1.3, 2.1
Convention of Language	1.b, 6.a, 6.d	2.16, 3.12, 3.13, 4.15		3.1, 4.2
Audio Quality	1.b, 6.a, 6.d	2.16, 3.21, 4.21		3.1, 4.2, 5.1, 5.2

Unit 13

Youth Radio

This unit is based on the work of Youth Radio (www.youthradio.org), one of the inspirations for the podcasting course I developed for NJeSchool. Youth Radio develops and disseminates compelling audio productions by young people on cultural, political, and social issues. The segments mix memoir, interviews, and journalistic reporting into fascinating segments lasting anywhere between 2 and 10 minutes. Before I discovered podcasting, I would simply enjoy listening to the segments on my local NPR station, wistfully imagining the educational potential of a recording studio to produce such segments with high school students. When I got the first version of iTunes that supported podcasting, I immediately began to download Youth Radio and listened to dozens of segments with an eye toward having students become consumers, creators, and critics.

SUMMARY

Students will record a Youth Radio–style feature where they connect the personal interests and experiences of youth with larger social, political, and cultural phenomena.

GRADE LEVELS

Grades 7–12

OBJECTIVES

- Synthesize personal experience with social issues
- Employ effective techniques of spoken language
- Organize ideas in an effective way
- Use the material of others ethically and effectively

TIME ALLOWANCE

4–7 days

RESOURCES

At least one computer with multitrack audio editing software and a microphone

Youth Radio: www.youthradio.org

Youth Radio has some helpful suggestions for media production:
www.youthradio.org/fourthr/productiontechniques.shtml

Procedures

Listen to a variety of Youth Radio segments with your students (see Examples section, next page).

Use the following questions in discussions with your students:

1. Each of these stories has a unique point of view and an opinion. Are there any elements or ideas that you strongly agree with? Disagree with? Are confused about?

2. Which stories would you consider to be about political or social issues? Why? What does it mean to have a social or political theme in a story?

3. All of the radio essays connect a personal experience with bigger issues. Describe and analyze this connection. How do the speakers connect their personal experiences to larger issues?

4. What audio effects, quotes, interviews, and music did each of these essays use? How were they used, and what effect did they have on you as a listener? Did these additions enhance or detract from the author's story?

You should then brainstorm with students on social, cultural, or political issues, as well as on personal issues—many of which have unrecognized but powerful connections to the larger phenomena.

Students will write a draft of the text that they will use, including notations of where interviews, music, and/or sound effects will be used. Students may organize their work in a variety of ways, but there should be a focus on communicating the main issues and eliciting an emotional connection to the listeners.

Review each student's transcript before they begin recording.

Examples

"That Sickening Smell?"
www.youthradio.org/environmental/061205_air.shtml

> Youth Radio's Sophie Simon-Ortiz grew up in West Berkeley near a steel manufacturing plant, and she still has vivid memories of the smell that poured regularly from its smoke stacks and permeated the neighborhood. The smell is still there. So Sophie decided to find out why, after so many years and complaints by nearby residents, not much seems to have changed at all.

"The Beef"
www.youthradio.org/lifestyle/kcbs070715_beef.shtml

> In response to animal cruelty, Youth Radio's Catlin Grey became vegan. She and her mom often stressed about what was cooking in the kitchen. She says, "I thought that my yearning for cheddar cheese and cookie dough ice cream would be my biggest challenge. But it turned out to be my mom."

"MySpace vs. Facebook"
www.youthradio.org/society/kcbs071028_myspace.shtml

> Youth Radio reporter Leon Sykes describes his life as social networking junkie and his use of MySpace and Facebook to express himself online. "They're like the left and right side of my brain."

"Living with PTSD"
www.youthradio.org/reflections/npr051123_ptsd.shtml

> Jesus Bocanegra, now 23, spent 4½ years in the military, including a year as a cavalry scout in Iraq. He's now out of the military and living with his family in the town of Elsep in south Texas. But the war is still with him, so much so that he's been treated for post-traumatic stress disorder. He shares this story.

Rubric for Unit 13: Youth Radio

	Exemplary	Satisfactory	Unsatisfactory
Content of Recording	Strong connection between personal experiences and social issues	Connection between personal experiences and social issues	No/little connection between personal experiences and social issues
Narration	Clear and paced spoken language throughout and effective use of spoken techniques in recording	General concern for clarity, pace, and spoken techniques	Little concern for clarity, pace, or spoken techniques (inflection, tone, pauses, etc.)
Organization of Recording	Ideas are consistently organized and presented in an effective way	Ideas are generally organized and presented in an effective way	Ideas are not organized or presented in an effective way
Language in Recording	Effective use of stylistic techniques (e.g., figurative language, transitions, varied sentence types)	Use of stylistic techniques (e.g., figurative language, transitions, varied sentence types)	Inappropriate or lack of stylistic techniques (e.g., figurative language, transitions, varied sentence types)
Citations of Music and Sound Effects Resources	Clear credit of resources in audio file from appropriate sources—listener can easily find source material, Creative Commons material, or student can justify fair use	Attempt to credit resources used, audio and resources are from appropriate sources—Creative Commons material or student can justify fair use	No citations of audio or inappropriate audio used or student unable to justify fair use
Legal and Ethical Guidelines	All course rules are followed consistently through the process	Course rules are followed for final production, but minor deviations occur during process	Repeated or significant violations of course rule throughout process

(continued)

Rubric for Unit 13: Youth Radio *(continued)*

	Related NETS·S	Related IRA/NCTE Standards	Related AASL Standards	Related TESOL Standard	Related Social Studies Standards	Related WIDA Standards
Content of Recording	1.a, 1.b, 2.b	7	1.1.1, 1.1.2, 2.1.1, 3.1.5, 3.3.4, 4.4.1		1, 4	1, 2, 5— Writing 1, 2, 5— Speaking
Narration		4, 5, 6		1.1, 2.2, 3,1		1, 2, 5— Speaking 2, 5— Writing
Organization of Recording		4, 5, 6	2.1.1, 2.2.2	1.3, 3.3		
Language in Recording		4, 5, 6				1, 2— Speaking
Citations of Music and Sound Effects Resources	3.b, 5.a	4, 8	1.3.1, 1.3.3, 1.3.5, 3.1.6, 4.3.4			1—Speaking 1—Writing
Legal and Ethical Guidelines	5.a, 6.a		1.3.1, 1.3.3, 1.3.5, 3.1.6, 4.3.4			

Unit 14

Historical
Interview

This unit was inspired by the work of Ken Burns, particularly his most recent project *The War* (www.pbs.org/thewar/). In *The War* Ken Burns focuses on four towns in the United States during World War II—on the soldiers who went to fight and the people who stayed behind. It is Burns's focus on social history and especially on the perspectives of people who have been previously marginalized in historical accounts that is often the most interesting. This unit was also inspired by StoryCorps (www.storycorps.net), a nonprofit initiative to record, preserve, and share the stories of everyday people. StoryCorps is especially powerful because it provides anyone with the tools, techniques, and opportunities to interview the people closest to them.

Women War Workers, 1942. Courtesy of the National Archives and Records Administration

For this project students will interview someone they know about experiences during an interesting time period or a historic event. The people interviewed do not have to have been directly involved in the historic event. People's indirect experiences—as bystanders or witnesses—can be just as powerful. The interview can cover more than a single event. For example, telling of living in the South during segregation or growing up on a farm can create extremely powerful interviews.

SUMMARY

Students will record a StoryCorps-style interview with someone they know who has lived through an interesting time period or historic event. Students place the interview within a larger historical context by including appropriate historical information before, after, or during the interview.

GRADE LEVELS

Grades 5–12

OBJECTIVES

- Cultivate an interesting story from a person's experience
- Research historical background
- Integrate personal experiences with historical research
- Effectively produce interview
- Use the material of others ethically and effectively

TIME ALLOWANCE

3 days to 2 weeks

RESOURCES

At least one computer with multitrack audio editing software and a microphone

Ken Burns's *The War*. www.pbs.org/thewar/

Eighty-seven-year-old Kay Wang tells her granddaughter, Chen, and her son, Cheng, about her childhood. www.storycorps.net/listen/stories/kay-wang

Ray Martinez remembers growing up in an orphanage during the 1950s. www.storycorps.net/listen/stories/ray-martinez

Carly Dreher interviews her grandfather Lyle Link, who is 90, about growing up on his family's farm. www.storycorps.net/listen/stories/lyle-link-and-carly-dreher

Ella Owens tells her daughter, Lynn Reed, about participating in a march during the 1968 Memphis Sanitation Workers' Strike. www.storycorps.net/listen/stories/ella-annette-owens

Procedures

Give students the following directions:

1. Pick a family member or friend to interview.

2. Ask him or her to briefly tell you about four or five interesting events from his or her life.

3. Choose one event or experience to focus on.

4. Develop interview questions.

5. Interview the person and record the interview.

6. Research and provide information about the larger historical context of the interview topic.

7. Decide how much of the historical information to include and where.

8. Edit the interview after your recording.

9. Cite your sources.

Here are some guidelines to help your students conduct better interviews. These guidelines are modified from Youth Radio's Production Techniques (www.youthradio.org/fourthr/productiontechniques.shtml):

- When conducting interviews, remember to follow the classroom guidelines (see Appendix A).

- Start with "easy" questions to build a comfort level with your interviewee.

- Avoid yes/no questions.

- Have a checklist of items that you'd like to cover with your interviewee.

- Don't worry too much about your interviewee getting off topic. Some interesting stories might come up, and you can always edit out any uninteresting material.

Example

Here are several examples of the historic interview project:

http://podcourse.blogspot.com/historic-interview.htm

Rubric for Unit 14: Historical Interview

	Exemplary	Satisfactory	Unacceptable
Listener Interest	Regardless of topic or person interviewed, the interview was an interesting personal story	The interview was generally interesting	Little concern for audience interest
Context	Appropriate historical information was provided and cited	Historical information provided, but either too much or too little, and properly cited	No/inappropriate historical information provided or no citations
Interview Techniques	Consistently allowed and guided interviewee to tell interesting and personal story connected to historic events or social history	Generally allowed interviewee to tell interesting and personal story connected to historic events or social history	Failed to allow interview to tell interesting and personal story connected to historic events or social history
Recording Quality	All voices clearly audible throughout	Voices generally audible throughout	Frequent problems hearing interview
Citations of Music and Sound Effects Resources	Clear credit of resources in audio file from appropriate sources—listener can easily find source material, Creative Commons material, or student can justify fair use	Attempt to credit resources used, audio and resources are from appropriate sources—Creative Commons material or student can justify fair use	No citations of audio or inappropriate audio used or student unable to justify fair use
Legal and Ethical Guidelines	All course rules are followed consistently through the process	Course rules are followed for final production, but minor deviations occur during process	Repeated or significant violations of course rule throughout process

(continued)

Rubric for Unit 14: Historical Interview (continued)

	Related NETS·S	Related IRA/NCTE Standards	Related AASL Standards	Related TESOL Standard	Related Social Studies Standards	Related WIDA Standards
Listener Interest	1.a, 1.b	7	2.3.1			1, 5— Speaking 1, 5— Writing
Context	3.b	3, 7	1.1.4, 2.1.1	2.2	1, 2, 3, 4	5—Speaking 5—Writing
Interview Techniques		1, 2, 3, 4, 7	1.1.3, 1.1.4, 1.1.9, 1.1.2, 2.1.1, 3.3.2	1.1	1, 2, 3, 4	1, 5— Speaking 1, 5— Writing
Recording Quality		4	3.1.3	3.1		
Citations of Music and Sound Effects Resources	3.b, 5.a	4, 8	1.3.1, 1.3.3, 1.3.5, 3.1.6, 4.3.4			1—Speaking 1—Writing
Legal and Ethical Guidelines	5.a, 6.a		1.3.1, 1.3.3, 1.3.5, 3.1.6, 4.3.4			

Unit 15

By Kathleen Jerome

Citizen
Journalists

During the 2007–2008 school year, while finishing up my master's degree, I was substitute teaching at a nearby elementary school of about 500 students. For my thesis, I wanted to support a curriculum unit using podcasting. I didn't have a classroom, I didn't have school equipment, and I didn't have students. I borrowed a classroom. I loaded my laptop with Audacity, bought a cheap microphone (Radio Shack, $10), and decided to run a journalism podcasting club.

I planned a radio news show for fifth and sixth graders that would increase their social skills, give them a voice (Gordon, 2007), and increase collaboration skills (Ormrod, 2006). I could also fulfill several of our state curriculum content standards for technology, literacy, and social studies. I researched journalism, practiced podcasting (which was not so difficult), got permission from administrators and parents, and organized the lessons.

All went well! The students did not want to stop reporting. They were very excited about hearing their voices. One of the students even created a podcast at home for one class project. After we finished this journalism show, the school began a school newspaper using desktop publishing, which had not been envisioned before. Although they were not using podcasting, journalism and technology had been introduced.

SUMMARY

In groups, students become journalists, writing and recording a feature story and interviewing someone in connection with the story to create a finished podcast.

GRADE LEVELS

Grades 5–6

OBJECTIVES

- Write program scripts
- Research appropriate topics
- Use effective techniques of spoken language
- Listen effectively to peer's work
- Provide constructive feedback on peer's work

TIME ALLOWANCE

Two weeks to entire school semester

RESOURCES

At least one computer with multitrack audio editing software and a microphone

I found the following websites to be very helpful in finding information about journalism and forming journalism clubs or newspapers.

Web English Teacher website
www.webenglishteacher.com/journ.html.

Beginning Reporting website by Jim Hall
http://www.courses.vcu.edu/ENG-jeh/BeginningReporting/

Franklin School Journalism club guide
www.cdschool.org/cocurricular/NESPA/
BeginninganElementarySchoolJournalismClub2007.pdf

These are just a few of the many sites available on the Internet. The amount of useful information was quite stunning, so you can explore yourself if you have more specific goals.

Procedures

Here are the general steps it takes to run a journalism podcasting unit.

Permissions

The very first thing you must do is make sure that podcasting fits in with your school's Acceptable Use Policy (AUP). You must hand out any necessary permission slips and tell students that those slips must be signed and turned in before they or any interviewee has their voice uploaded to the Internet.

Journalism

The students will want to dive right in, interviewing everyone willy-nilly, with no permissions or forethought. The first session, therefore, has to be about prewriting and researching. Since the students are learning about journalism, review types of journalism articles and roles that students will play in the podcasting process. Review copyright and the rules for interviewing (no secret interviews, interviewee must give permission). Some of the article types and roles I have used are:

- Features Reporter—interviews with teacher of the week
- Sports Reporter—cover school sports event
- News of the school
- Entertainment—reviews of current movies, etc.

Have students form writing groups according to interest. In the event that all the students want to report on sports or interview teachers, you can set this up on a rotating basis. Once students write their own stories, you will review them before recording.

Recording

Let two students demonstrate an unplanned interview while you record. When you play the recording, students will be able to see that it did not come out very well. Now have the students plan an interview with you; they must set up the questions and get your permission. The next step is to have students plan their interviews with their intended subjects, get the subjects' permission, and record their interviews.

The students must take turns recording, working on a separate project while other students are using the computer. If there is more than one computer, several groups may record at once, as long as the noise does not interfere with the other groups. Once all the recordings have been made and saved, editing will begin.

Classroom Management

Even with planning, students sometimes get disruptive. If they are bored or someone is left without a job, things get loud. I experimented with different techniques, and these worked the best for me.

- Clearly delineated tasks. It is not enough to say, "Write your article and record it." It is better to be very specific. For example: "You want to write a story that is approximately five sentences. You want your audience to be interested, but not to have so long a story that they get bored. Make sure you answer the pertinent journalism questions of who, what, when, where and why."

- Roles to play within the activity (you can even assign one student the role of moderator). If Susie knows she is the MC, and Robert knows he is the sports reporter, and Jane knows she is the recording technician, then things run much more smoothly.

- Handouts that students can refer to, so that they can do the tasks without having to ask repeatedly how to do them and can feel that they are doing them themselves.

- Create alternative activities for those students not recording or editing. Whether it's a packet or a poster, or a paper or a journal, students must have something to do if they are not the team recording. (All the students want to record all the time, so the process must be managed.)

- No "scoot overs." If there are students who "take over," it is extremely disruptive. I call this the "scoot-over rule." No one was allowed to say, "I know how to do this—scoot over."

Example

Here is the site of the class newscast:

www.kljerometeach.com/newspage.html

Rubric for Unit 15: Citizen Journalists

	Exemplary	Satisfactory	Unacceptable
Program Script	Writing is clear and concise. There are minimal spelling and grammatical errors in the script	There are some spelling and grammatical errors in the script	Writing is unclear, incomplete. There are many grammatical and spelling errors in the script
Subject Matter Covered	Student chose a suitable journalism topic	Student chose a topic that did not require research or was too narrow	There was no research. The student read from a book or article that they didn't write
Podcast Presentation	Spoke clearly and loudly. Presentation expressed understanding of the information	Some sections difficult to hear or understand, but understandable as a whole. Could improve with practice	Presentation unclear and not thought through, or incomplete. Minimal effort expended
Podcast Creation	Understood basics of recording, uploading and burning a podcast. Could edit or rerecord podcast as needed	Understood basics of podcasting. Rerecorded if sound too low	Podcast unclear or difficult to hear. Not all steps completed. Did not understand what podcasting entailed
Listening	Listened and made comments to other student podcasts. Joined in the discussion	Listened, but made minimal input	Did not pay attention
Legal and Ethical Guidelines	All course rules are followed consistently through the process	Course rules are followed for final production, but minor deviations occur during process	Repeated or significant violations of course rule throughout process

(continued)

Rubric for Unit 15: Citizen Journalists *(continued)*

	Related NETS·S	Related IRA/NCTE Standards	Related AASL Standards	Related TESOL Standard	Related Social Studies Standards	Related WIDA Standards
Program Script	1.b, 4.a, 6.a, 6.d	3, 5, 7	1.2.1, 1.2.4, 2.1.1, 2.1.2, 2.1.3, 2.3.1, 4.1.3	1.2, 1.3, 2.2, 2.3, 3.3		1, 2, 5— Writing
Subject Matter Covered	1.b, 3.a, 3.c, 4.a, 5.d, 6.d	3, 5, 7	1.2.4, 1.2.7, 1.3.2, 2.1.3, 2.3.1	1.2, 1.3, 2.2, 2.3, 3.3	1, 3	1, 2, 5— Writing
Podcast Presentation	1.b, 6.a, 6.d	4, 11, 12	1.1.9, 2.1.6, 3.2.1, 3.1.1, 3.3.5, 3.4.4, 4.3.1	3.1		1, 2, 5— Speaking
Podcast Creation	2.a, 2.b, 2.d, 6.a, 6.b, 6.d	7, 8, 11	1.1.8, 2.1.6, 2.3.1	2.2		1, 2, 5— Speaking Writing
Listening	2.a, 5.b	11	3.2.2, 3.3.3	3.2		1, 2, 5— Listening
Legal and Ethical Guidelines	5.a, 6.a		1.3.1, 1.3.3, 1.3.5, 3.1.6, 4.3.4			

Works Cited

Franklin School. (2007). Franklin School journalism club: A step-by-step guide. Retrieved August 6, 2008, from www.cdschool.org/cocurricular/NESPA/BeginninganElementarySchoolJournalismClub2007.pdf

Gordon, A. (2007). Booklinks: Sound off! The possibilities of podcasting. Retrieved October 17, 2007, from www.ala.org/booklinks

Hall, J. (n.d.). Beginning reporting. Retrieved August 6, 2008 from www.courses.vcu.edu/ENG-jeh/BeginningReporting/.

Ormrod, J. (2006). *Educational psychology, developing learners* (5th ed.). Upper Saddle River, NJ: Pearson Prentice Hall.

Web English Teacher. (2008). Journalism resources. Retrieved August 6, 2008 from www.webenglishteacher.com/journ.html

Unit 16

Director's Cut
DVD
Commentary

For this project students will create an audio recording to accompany a scene from a movie. Audio commentary that runs concurrently with a movie is a genre of podcasting as well as a popular feature of many DVDs.

Students can collaborate with friends, family, or community members. Films that work well with this project, especially if students worked with a person with experience during these time periods, are *Slaughterhouse 5*, *Mississippi Burning*, *Born on the Fourth of July*, *Apocalypse Now*, *Forest Gump*, *Valley Girl*, and *Wall Street*. In this way students get to interact with family members and friends as well as the larger community of fans of that movie. It is an excellent example of the flow of ideas through different media and participatory culture (Jenkins, 2006).

SUMMARY

Students create an informational or critical recording that will run synchronously with a particular scene of a movie. The listener cues the movie to a particular point and is able to hear the audio commentary of the student.

GRADE LEVELS

Grades 5–12

OBJECTIVES

- Synchronize original audio with movie
- Use spoken techniques effectively
- Conduct and present appropriate research
- Anticipate and address the interests of a particular audience
- Use the material of others ethically and effectively

TIME ALLOWANCE

7–14 days

RESOURCES

At least one computer with multitrack audio editing software and a microphone

Television and DVD player

Procedures

Below are the instructions given to students:

Your commentary should be 150–250 words and cover 4–6 minutes of the movie. You should begin by clearly instructing the viewer where to cue the movie. Your commentary will be synchronized with the movie. When providing facts about the movie, cross-check these facts with at least two sources, and cite any and all sources.

Below are four types of popular commentary. Your commentary should include at least three of them.

Factual

- Background—This commentary focuses on the plot of the movie. For example, information about the characters, setting, or historical time period of the movie.

- Context—This commentary focuses on the making of the movie. Is it based on a book? Who are the stars? What else were they in? Do you know if anything interesting happened while shooting the movie? Who is the director and what else did he/she direct?

Opinion

- Analysis—This is your opinion on the actions of the scene. For example, what is going on in this scene, and what should a viewer pay attention to? Do you agree or disagree with what the characters are doing? Are there any important details in this scene that you want to point out so a viewer doesn't miss them?

- Critique—This is your opinion on the making of the movie. For example, what parts of the scene did the actor and directors do well, and what parts do you think they do not do well? What went right or wrong?

Example

Here's an example of an expert commentary for a Harry Potter film.

http://podcourse.blogspot.com/2008/11/bonus-dvd.html

Rubric for Unit 16: Director's Cut DVD Commentary

	Exemplary	Satisfactory	Unacceptable
Synchronization	Content of audio correlates to action on screen all/most of the time	Content of audio correlates to action on screen some of the time	Content of audio correlates to action on screen little/none of the time
Voice	Clear and engaging. Speaker sounds interested in material and eager to share knowledge with viewer	Clear and somewhat engaging. Speaker generally communicates interest to listener	Difficulty hearing speaker *or* dull/monotonous delivery
Facts	All factual statements are valid and have been checked with at least two sources	Most facts are valid and have most have been checked with at least two sources	Significant number of facts are inaccurate and have not been checked
Listener Interest	All/most commentary and opinions would be interesting to both a new viewer and a fan of the movie	All/most of the commentary and opinions would be interesting to either a new viewer or a fan of the movie	Significant amount of commentary and opinions would not be interesting to either a new viewer or a fan of the movie
Citations of Music and Sound Effects Resources	Clear credit of resources in audio file from appropriate sources—listener can easily find source material, Creative Commons material, or student can justify fair use	Attempt to credit resources used, audio and resources are from appropriate sources—Creative Commons material or student can justify fair use	No citations of audio or inappropriate audio used or student unable to justify fair use
Legal and Ethical Guidelines	All course rules are followed consistently through the process	Course rules are followed for final production, but minor deviations occur during process	Repeated or significant violations of course rule throughout process

(continued)

Rubric for Unit 16: Director's Cut DVD Commentary *(continued)*

	Related NETS·S	Related IRA/NCTE Standards	Related AASL Standards	Related TESOL Standard	Related Social Studies Standards*	Related WIDA Standards
Synchronization	1.a 1.b, 2.b	1, 2, 3, 4	2.1.2, 2.1.6, 3.1.3			
Voice		6	3.1.3	1.1, 3.1		1—Speaking 1—Reading
Facts			1.1.1, 1.2.2, 1.2.3, 2.1.1, 3.1.1	2.2	1, 2, 3, 4	1, 2, 5—Reading
Listener Interest		5	1.1.2	1.1		1—Writing 1—Speaking
Citations of Music and Sound Effects Resources	3.b, 5.a	4, 8	1.3.1, 1.3.3, 1.3.5, 3.1.6, 4.3.4			1—Speaking 1—Writing
Legal and Ethical Guidelines	5.a, 6.a		1.3.1, 1.3.3, 1.3.5, 3.1.6, 4.3.4			

Social Studies Standards can be addressed if the teacher modified this project to target the historical or cultural study of a film.

Works Cited

Jenkins, H. (2006). *Confronting the challenges of participatory culture: Media education for the 21st century.* Boston: MacArthur Foundation. Retrieved July 7, 2008, from http://newmedialiteracies.org/files/working/NMLWhitePaper.pdf

Unit 17

Student-Run
Podcasts

Up to this point, the units have focused on individual podcast episodes. This final unit provides directions for students to create their own ongoing podcasts.

SUMMARY

Students create their own ongoing podcast according to their interests.

GRADE LEVELS

Grades 3–12

OBJECTIVES

- To reflect, develop, focus, and expand upon student interests.

- To create a production to entertain and inform a specific audience

- To synthesize facts and ideas from multiple sources

- To demonstrate technical proficiency in the medium of audio mixing

- To use clear, varied, and appropriate standard English

- To sustain, adapt, and modify an existing plan

- To use metadata effectively

- To internalize the process of ethically using the intellectual property of others to create original content

TIME ALLOWANCE

3 weeks to entire school year

RESOURCES

At least one computer with multitrack audio editing software and a microphone

Other resources may be required depending on the podcast topic chosen

Procedures

The following are the main procedures for scaffolding students in making their own podcasts. They are built on the previous work in this book. Your students should be familiar with Appendix A: Legal and Ethical Considerations for Student Podcasters; Appendix C: Podcasting Rules for the Classroom (or your version); and the technologies of creating an mp3 and the resources to syndicate it (Blip.tv, Switchpod, etc.)—all information in the beginning chapters.

For the content, you can use or modify ideas from the previous units or have students do work based on other popular formats (listed below). I would recommend giving students control over the focus of their shows.

Below are the instructions for your students:

Choose a focus, audience, and name for your podcast. Your show could be on a specific topic or just "Things That Interest You." Here are possible topics.

- Sports
- Fitness
- Fashion News
- Comic Books
- Teen Interests
- Disney
- Movies and Television
- Celebrity News
- Environmental Issues
- Technology
- Video Games
- Science
- Politics
- Current Events

You should look at iTunes (www.itunes.com) and Podcast.com (www.podcast.com) to get ideas for your podcast topic and name. (If you are unfamiliar with iTunes, you should know that it is an Internet-based software program that you have to download and install on your computer. It's a big program and can slow down older computers. You might want to simply look at Podcast.com.) You should also review the Legal and Ethical Considerations for Student Podcasters and Podcasting Rules for the Classroom.

You will need to submit a description of the show and a name for the show. The show should briefly describe who would be interested in listening, what you will cover, and why people should listen. Remember, your podcast will be broadcast around the world!

Your individual shows can be any one of the following formats, or you can combine formats (or come up with something of your own). For example, if you are doing a show about comic books, you can do three shows that review different comics, or you can do a show that's a news report on new comics, a show that's an interview with a friend who collects comics, and a show that gives advice on how to buy and take care of comics.

Here are some suggested formats:

- News report—unbiased reporting some current event
- Commentary—your opinion on an event
  (sports, news, movie, TV show, celebrities, fashion)
- Advice/Instructions/How-to
- Reviews—TV show, video game, movie
- Interviews—Friends, family, or community members
  (get parental permission and follow podcasting rules)
- Audio tour of an important place
- DVD commentary

You should create a schedule for your podcast episodes.

Task for Students	Description and Comments for Teachers	Due Dates
Brainstorm title	Remind the students to make it interesting	
Write one-paragraph description	You should ask the students what the focus of the show will be, who the audience will be, and why the audience will want to listen	
Outline the first three episodes	The students should briefly describe the first three episodes—this can be changed, but they need a starting point	
Plan and record first episode	See formats	
Plan and record second episode	See formats	
Make it public for the world to see	Share the information from Chapter 2 on RSS feeds and podcast hosting services, if you have not done so already	
Plan and record third episode	See formats	

Examples

Youth Radio
www.youthradio.org

> Podcasts on issues by and for young people.

Shambles.net
www.shambles.net/pages/learning/infolit/studentpod/

> A directory of podcasts from international schools.

Alaska Teen Media Institute
www.alaskateenmedia.org

> Provides Alaskan teens with the tools and training needed to produce stories—told in their own voices—to be shared through a variety of media.

Appalachia Media Institute
www.appalshop.org/ami/

> Young people in central Appalachia document the unique traditions and complex issues of their mountain communities.

Blunt Radio
www.bluntradio.org

> Weekly call-in show run by free and incarcerated teenagers in the Portland, Maine, area.

Rubric for Unit 17: Student-Run Podcasts

This rubric should be used in conference during the production process with students as well as a final evaluation.

	Exemplary	Satisfactory	Unacceptable
Focus	Show has a consistent, yet possibly evolving, focus that can be articulated by student and evident in all episodes	Show generally has a consistent theme; changes and evolutions somewhat explained to audience and teacher	Show lacks focus *or* changes not explained to teacher and audience
Audience	A genuine concern for the interests and background knowledge of the intended audience and engagement with audience	General consideration of the interests and background knowledge of target audience	Lack of a target audience(s) or a lack of consideration in the interests and background of target audience
Substance	Significant facts are substantiated by multiple sources	Most significant facts are substantiated by one or more sources	Significant facts frequently used without substantiation or citation
Mix	Seamless technical mix of music, external sound clips, and voices with infrequent or minor problems	General technical proficiency with audio mixing with some problems	Consistent errors in technical mix (e.g., volume, transitions, silences)
Language	Clear, varied, and appropriate use of standard English with minor deviations	Generally clear, appropriate, and varied use of standard English with some deviations	Lack of clear, appropriate, and varied use of standard English

(continued)

Rubric for Unit 17: Student-Run Podcasts *(continued)*

	Exemplary	Satisfactory	Unacceptable
Episodes	Appropriate and consistent episodes; any changes are clearly explained, format guidelines are followed, modifications are explained in conference with teacher	Episodes are generally consistent and follow format guidelines, changes in focus and formats are somewhat explained to audience and teacher	Episodes are inconsistent and inexplicably deviate from format guidelines
Metadata	Show and episode description, image, and feed information clear and easily accessible	Show and episode information are present and generally clear	Show and episode information inconsistent or unclear
Citations of Music and Sound Effects Resources	Clear credit of resources in audio file from appropriate sources—listener can easily find source material, Creative Commons material, or student can justify fair use	Attempt to credit resources used, audio and resources are from appropriate sources—Creative Commons material or student can justify fair use	No citations of audio or inappropriate audio used or student unable to justify fair use
Legal and Ethical Guidelines	All course rules are followed consistently through the process	Course rules are followed for final production, but minor deviations occur during process	Repeated or significant violations of course rule throughout process

(continued)

Rubric for Unit 17: Student-Run Podcasts *(continued)*

	Related NETS•S	Related IRA/NCTE Standards	Related AASL Standards	Related TESOL Standard	Related WIDA Standards
Focus	1.a, 1.b, 4.b, 5.d, 6.a	4, 5	1.1.2, 1.2.2	1.2	1—Writing 1—Speaking
Audience	2.b, 4.a	4, 5, 6, 11	2.3.1, 4.1.5	1.1	
Substance	3.a, 3.b, 4.c	4, 7	1.1.4, 1.2.1, 2.1.1	2.3	1, 2—Writing 1, 2—Speaking
Mix	6.a, 6.b, 6.c				
Language		4, 5, 6	2.1.6, 3.1.3	1.2, 3.1	1, 2—Speaking
Episodes		4, 6	1.1.2, 1.2.2	1.2	1—Writing 1—Speaking
Metadata		4, 5, 6	3.1.3		1, 2—Writing
Citations of Music and Sound Effects Resources	3.b, 5.a	4, 8	1.3.1, 1.3.3, 1.3.5, 3.1.6, 4.3.4		1—Speaking 1—Writing
Legal and Ethical Guidelines	5.a, 6.a		1.3.1, 1.3.3, 1.3.5, 3.1.6, 4.3.4		

Appendix A

Legal and Ethical Considerations for
Student Podcasters

This appendix shares my experiences and research working with podcasting and digital media in education. The three biggest legal and ethical issues that you will face as you teach podcasting are (1) issues related to student security online, (2) issues related to consent for recording, and (3) issues relating to copyright. This chapter looks chiefly at the issues of copyright, but I will address the other two as well.

In my podcasting course, the main way that I deal with the issue of security and safety is by prohibiting students from using any identifying information in their podcasts—no names, no addresses, no usernames (see Appendix C: Podcasting Rules for the Classroom for more). This rule goes for what students say about either themselves or others. I also prohibit anonymous slurs or gossip (this has never been an issue with my students). Most schools will address this issue in the acceptable use policies and have addressed similar issues with student web pages, newspapers, and web-based writing portfolios. Also, this topic is the focus of federal and state laws, so it is the one that most districts have policies and experience with.

The second major issue with student podcasting is the issue of consent. I address the issue of consent with a simple rule—students must get the permission of the person they record in an interview and let the interviewee know that he or she is being recorded and that this recording will be publicly available on the web.

In my class I strictly prohibited secret recordings. Although states vary on the legality of secret recordings, it is obviously an area ripe for mischief. However, I do discuss the ethical implications of secretly recording people: when it might be ethical (in an undercover journalism piece, for example) and when and why it would not be ethical. I would like to encourage you to have this discussion with your students, but stick to my policy. Keep in mind that many situations when secret recordings would be ethical would also be dangerous, so I would completely avoid having students do it.

Copyright and Podcasting

The issues of copyright and digital media are the most nuanced and common legal and ethical issues with student podcasting. Which music, audio, and readings created by other people can students include in their podcasts? A groundbreaking report by the Center for Social Media (Hobbs, Jaszi, & Aufderheide, 2007), *The Cost of Copyright Confusion for Media Literacy*, finds that confusion about copyright law in education has debilitating consequences for educators: "Teachers use less effective teaching techniques, teach and transmit erroneous copyright information, fail to share innovative instructional approaches, and do not take advantage of new digital platforms" (p. 1). The following information attempts to clarify some of the confusion about copyright, fair use, and digital media so you can maximize the educational uses of other people's work.

I would also like to encourage, even challenge, teachers to use troublesome and ambiguous issues of copyright and fair use as "teachable moments." Teaching students to be reflective and thoughtful appliers of fair use is a skill that will help them to continue to think about issues of individual rights and public interests.

Jane's Podcast Dilemma

Jane is a 16-year-old student with a very successful podcast. Though she started it only five months ago, Feedburner lists her podcast feed as having more than 500 subscribers. Her show is a mix of music and movie reviews, updates on her life, interviews, and opinions on current events.

Several times she has used sounds from popular music and movies in her podcast. Her introduction song is a clip from a popular song, and in her reviews she occasionally inserts clips of popular songs. She was vaguely aware of copyright laws. When she started, she had a small show that only her friends listened to, so she didn't bother to worry about it.

Now, she is getting offers from advertisers to put commercials on her podcast and on her homepage. She is also thinking about selling t-shirts on her site. As the listeners and interests grow, she doesn't want legal problems to jeopardize her show. She wonders what she can use legally without getting permission and what she needs to get permission for. What should Jane do?

The Beginning of the Answer...

The easy answer is that Jane needs to get permission from the rights holder for whatever music or sounds that she uses. The rights holders are not necessarily the bands, songwriters, or singers, but are likely the music companies that produce the music—the artist who made the music probably sold the rights to the company. There are also two parts to any song—the lyrics and music and the actual recording. She would need permission to use either. For example, she could not sing the song herself or broadcast the actual recording without getting permission from the person who owns the rights to the lyrics.

She would also need to get the rights for any material that she read on the podcast. For example, if she liked an article in the *New York Times*, she could not read the whole article on her podcast without getting permission.

However, Jane Should Know That...

U.S. copyright law allows for something called fair use. Fair use allows people to use other people's material (print, music, images) in certain cases without getting their permission. To decide whether your use falls under fair use, you need to consider four interrelated factors:

- The purpose and character of the use (How are you going to use the work? Fair use favors criticism, commentary, satire, and educational purposes.)

- The nature of the copyrighted work (What kind of work is it? It is much easier to claim fair use for facts like the weather or scientific information.)

- The amount and substantiality of the portion taken (What parts are you taking? Fair use favors small amounts, unimportant sections or parts.)

- The effect of the use upon the potential market (Will anyone lose money owed them if you copy and play this? Of course, fair use favors copying in which no one would lose money.)

So if Jane wanted to read a small portion of a *New York Times* article, if she wanted to read parts of it to criticize or comment on it, or if she wanted to write a funny and satirical version of the article, she could probably do this without permission and claim fair use. Only a judge can officially decide fair use.

If your invocation of fair use involves the Internet and there is a dispute with the rights holder, there are a variety of steps that occur to resolve the issue before this dispute would even reach a court as provided for by the Digital Millennium Copyright Act. The chief course begins with a request to take down the material from the Internet. The fairness of this option has been debated, but that is how these conflicts typically begin and end.

You should avoid relying on strict rules about the amount or types of material that you can use. Popular guidelines that offer such advice typically represent the most conservative interpretations of fair use. The actual law is intentionally more ambiguous.

For example, there are also "Guidelines for the Fair Use of Multimedia" that were developed in 1996 by the Conference on Fair Use, which specify limits for the educational use of video, audio, and images without receiving permission from the rights holder (e.g., 3 minutes of a movie, 30 seconds of a song) (University of Texas, 2001). These guidelines, though not law, are in numerous policies in school districts and colleges, despite the fact that they are opposed by organizations such as the Association of Research Libraries, the American Library Association, the National Association of School Administrators, the National Education Association, the U.S. Catholic Conference, and the National Association of Independent Schools (Association of Research Libraries, 1997). Indeed, in response to these guidelines the Association of Research Libraries called on its members to "resist relying on any proposed code of conduct which may substantially or artificially constrain the full and appropriate application of fair use" (Association of Research Libraries, 2007).

As educators working with fair use, we do enjoy an extra special consideration—the "good faith defense." Steven McDonald, a lawyer specializing in copyright law, describes it this way:

> In terms of risk analysis, the "good faith Fair Use defense" (17 U.S.C. 504(c)(2)) provides a potent defense for nonprofit educational institutions and libraries that simply make an honest mistake when trying to interpret the vast gray area of Fair Use—no statutory damages can be awarded. In fact, the mere existence of that defense probably makes it considerably less likely that they would even be defendants in the first place. (Chronicle of Higher Education, 2004)

For more information on fair use, see the University of Texas's Fair Use of Copyrighted Materials (www.utsystem.edu/OGC/intellectualProperty/copypol2.htm) and the Creative Commons' Legal Guide for Podcasters (http://wiki.creativecommons.org/Podcasting_Legal_Guide).

So What Exactly Is Copyright?

Copyright, trademarks, and patents are three ways that intellectual property (songs, books, software, etc.) is legally protected. Copyright begins once an idea is expressed in a fixed form—a printed document, an e-mail message, a recorded song. Your essays, your podcasts, and Beyoncé's music are all equally protected by copyright. Copyright gives the creator exclusive rights to reproduce, make derivative works, or perform his or her material. Copyright does not apply to ideas, only to the expression of ideas. Copyright is automatic; you do not need to include the © symbol or register your work.

Copyright protections do not last indefinitely. Because of changing laws there is no single time period for the protection of all material. For works created after January 1, 1978, copyright extends to 70 years after the author's death. There are different time periods for works for hire, works before 1978, and unpublished works before 1978. When a copyright expires, the protected work passes into the public domain—free to be copied, published, manipulated, or printed by anyone. The creator of a work can choose to put his or her work in the public domain before the expiration of copyright. Additionally, works authored by the U.S. Government are not eligible for copyright protection. For a comprehensive description of a copyright holder's rights and a list of time limitations of copyrighted material, see the U.S. Copyright Office (2006, www.copyright.gov/circs/circl.html.).

Here are some important facts about copyright:

- Copyright means that the owner of the material has the right to reproduce, perform, or make derivative works from material.

- A derivative work is usually a sequel (like the Harry Potter series) or alternative version (like a mix of a song).

- The person who creates the work (book, podcast, recording, computer program) initially holds the copyright, but he or she can give or sell this right to others.

- As soon as a podcast is recorded or an idea is written down, it is copyrighted.

- There is no need for the © symbol on printed work or a warning on a broadcast to indicate that a work is copyright protected. You can add one yourself on your papers (just hit the Ctrl+Alt+C keys) or include a copyright warning in your own podcasts.

- Copyright protection does not last forever; the length changes based on changing laws, but as a rule of thumb, think 70 years after the author's death. If you are interested, check U.S. Copyright Office (www.copyright.gov/circs/circl.html.) for the exact details.

- A person cannot use the copyrighted work of another person without permission from the copyright holder...except if it falls under the fair use part of the copyright law.

- Fair use is the part of copyright law that allows for the use of copyrighted material with no permission required.

- There are four interrelated conditions to guide protection by fair use (www.copyright.gov/fls/fl102.html): (1) purpose and character of the use, (2) nature of the copyrighted work, (3) amount and substance of the portion used, (4) effect on the potential value of the copyrighted work.

What Is Copyleft?

Copyleft refers to the movement that offers an alternative to copyright and gives people greater access to use materials. One of the most noteworthy efforts of copyleft is Creative Commons (www.creativecommons.org). Through its website this initiative offers creators of intellectual property the ability to register their original works with a sliding scale of restrictions and permissions.

An author, photographer, or musician can license a work for noncommercial activities, with attribution, or for nonderivative works. For example, a photographer can allow others to use an image for nonderivative use in which the original image can be used, but not altered. Or, a musician can share a song with an attribution restriction; this will allow people to download, share, and even profit from it, but with credit to the original musician (see Creative Commons Licenses for more details, http://creativecommons.org/licenses/).

Podcasters should know that there are many music sites that license with Creative Commons. Magnatune (www.magnatune.com), Opsound (www.opsound.org), GarageBand (www.garageband.com), and Dance-Industries (www.dance-industries.com) all have original music with Creative Commons licenses. The Freesounds Project (http://freesound.iua.upf.edu) is an excellent source for sound effects (music is explicitly barred) with Creative Commons licenses. The Creative Commons Mixter (www.ccmixter.org) has music and audio samples (simple sound clips) and remixes using these sound clips. For many of the projects in this book, we used material with Creative Commons licenses.

A Good Answer for Jane...

Jane should invoke fair use when she is engaging in criticism or commentary and using small portions of works. If Jane wants to use music to enhance the production value of her show (say, for a theme song) she should use music files with appropriate Creative Commons licenses. If she chooses to use copyrighted music, she will need to get permission and likely pay a fee.

Works Cited

Association of Research Libraries. (1997). Association of Research Libraries: CCUMC multimedia fair use guidelines letter. Retrieved July 17, 2008, from www.arl.org/pp/ppcopyright/copyresources/ccumc.shtml

Association of Research Libraries. (2007). Association of Research Libraries: Conference on fair use joint statement. Retrieved July 17, 2008, from www.arl.org/pp/ppcopyright/copyresources/confu.shtml

Chronicle of Higher Education. (2004, July). The Chronicle: Colloquy live transcript. Retrieved February 21, 2008, from http://chronicle.com/colloquylive/2004/07/copyright/

Creative Commons. (2006). Podcasting legal guide—cc wiki. Retrieved February 21, 2008, from http://wiki.creativecommons.org/Podcasting_Legal_Guide

Hobbs, R., Jaszi, P., & Aufderheide, P. (2007, September). The cost of copyright confusion for media literacy. The Center for Social Media. Retrieved July 29, 2008, from www.centerforsocialmedia.org/resources/publications/the_cost_of_copyright_confusion_for_media_literacy

U.S. Copyright Office. (2006). Copyright office basics. Retrieved February 21, 2008, from www.copyright.gov/circs/circ1.html

University of Texas. (2001). Fair use guidelines for educational multimedia. Retrieved July 29, 2008 from www.utsystem.edu/OGC/intellectualProperty/ccmcguid.htm

University of Texas. (2005, March). Fair use of copyrighted materials. Retrieved February 21, 2008, from www.utsystem.edu/OGC/intellectualProperty/copypol2.htm

Appendix B

Copyright and
Fair Use Quiz for
Podcasting

I typically treat this quiz as an "errorless activity." There is no passing score except for 100%. If a student gets one wrong, he or she has to reread the material and take it over again. They cannot continue with podcasting until they answer every question correctly. You might want to modify it and require the students to give their rationales for their answers. See the answers on the next page.

Look at the fair use factors for the scenarios below. Do you consider these cases to be fair use?

1. A student creates a presentation for history class on the Vietnam War. In class she plays several songs from the time period. Is this fair use?

   a. Yes

   b. No

   c. Maybe

   d. Not an issue of copyright or fair use.

2. A student creates a website dedicated to his favorite band, Five for Fighting. On this website a user can download songs from the band's latest album. Is this fair use?

   a. Yes

   b. No

   c. Maybe

   d. Not an issue of copyright or fair use.

3. You use a clip from an Eminem song as the introduction and closing of your podcast. Is this fair use?

    a. Probably Yes

    b. Probably No

    c. Maybe

    d. Not an issue of copyright or fair use.

4. You record an English class where the students are reading and discussing the book *Of Mice and Men.* If you podcast this discussion, would this be fair use?

    a. Probably Yes

    b. Probably No

    c. Maybe

    d. Not an issue of copyright or fair use

5. On your podcast you make a satirical version of the movie Star Wars. You turn this adventure into a comedy. Fair use?

    a. Probably Yes

    b. Probably No

    c. Maybe

    d. Not an issue of copyright or fair use

6. A classmate of yours writes you an e-mail with an excellent description of the school. You like it so much that you read it on your podcast, without getting her permission. Fair use?

    a. Yes

    b. No

    c. Maybe

    d. Not an issue of copyright or fair use.

Answers to Copyright and Fair Use Quiz for Podcasting

1. *(a. Yes)* This is the reason why fair use was created, so that teachers and students can share information and content. This is a clear application of fair use.

2. *(b. No)* This is a clear violation of copyright law. The copyright holder has the right to distribute his or her work to make money; it is obvious that free downloads will harm sales. There is no application of fair use here.

3. *(b. Probably No)* It might be if you use a small clip, but I would strongly recommend avoiding it. Even if it's a small clip, if it's a very unique or recognizable riff or snippet, that involves the "substantiality" of the excerpt that you took.

4. *(a. Probably Yes)* The purpose of discussing books is a legitimate educational activity. It's natural and beneficial to quote parts of the book. This looks like fair use.

5. *(a. Probably Yes)* Thought fair use for satire has been invoked successfully and unsuccessfully, the more popular and powerful the original material is, the more it opens itself to satire.

6. *(b. No)* No matter if it's a famous author or your best friend, everyone's work is copyrighted once it hits a fixed form. You should respect the work of others and expect others to respect your ownership of your material.

Appendix C

Podcasting Rules for
the Classroom

I have used the following podcasting rules successfully in my podcasting classes. You may use these or modify them accordingly.

Below are the rules for the podcasting in this course. They are in addition to the school rules and policies.

1. **Appropriate Language.** No profanity or obscenities in the most general sense of the terms will be allowed in any format in this course—in projects or in communication with other students or the instructor.

2. **Safety for Self and Others.** You are not to mention personally identifying information on any audio broadcast or accompanying document that is intended for use outside of the course—this includes last names, screen names, school name, home address, or any other unique information about yourself or others.

3. **Respect for Others.** You should communicate with other students in the course with courtesy and respect. Disagreements are allowed but must be communicated in respectful language.

4. **Respect for Intellectual Property.** You may not use the intellectual property (audio, text, video, images, etc.) of another person without permission unless you can clearly explain and justify the invocation of fair use.

5. **Consent.** You need to get the permission of any person you intend to record and include in a podcast. This person should be informed that the recording is for the public and for your podcast. You must not use deception or record a person before you get his or her permission.

6. **Reciprocity.** You should also expect others—inside and outside of this course—to treat you according to these rules. It's not just about being nice—most of these rules correlate with state, federal, and international laws. For example, no one should take your original material without your permission.

For more information see the Podcasting Legal Guide at Creative Commons (http://wiki.creativecommons.org/Podcasting_Legal_Guide).

Appendix D

Standards
Referenced

National Educational Technology Standards for Students (NETS·S)

All K–12 students should be prepared to meet the following standards and performance indicators.

1. **Creativity and Innovation**

   Students demonstrate creative thinking, construct knowledge, and develop innovative products and processes using technology. Students:

   a. apply existing knowledge to generate new ideas, products, or processes

   b. create original works as a means of personal or group expression

   c. use models and simulations to explore complex systems and issues

   d. identify trends and forecast possibilities

2. Communication and Collaboration

Students use digital media and environments to communicate and work collaboratively, including at a distance, to support individual learning and contribute to the learning of others. Students:

- **a.** interact, collaborate, and publish with peers, experts, or others employing a variety of digital environments and media
- **b.** communicate information and ideas effectively to multiple audiences using a variety of media and formats
- **c.** develop cultural understanding and global awareness by engaging with learners of other cultures
- **d.** contribute to project teams to produce original works or solve problems

3. Research and Information Fluency

Students apply digital tools to gather, evaluate, and use information. Students:

- **a.** plan strategies to guide inquiry
- **b.** locate, organize, analyze, evaluate, synthesize, and ethically use information from a variety of sources and media
- **c.** evaluate and select information sources and digital tools based on the appropriateness to specific tasks
- **d.** process data and report results

4. Critical Thinking, Problem Solving, and Decision Making

Students use critical-thinking skills to plan and conduct research, manage projects, solve problems, and make informed decisions using appropriate digital tools and resources. Students:

- **a.** identify and define authentic problems and significant questions for investigation
- **b.** plan and manage activities to develop a solution or complete a project

    c. collect and analyze data to identify solutions and make informed decisions

    d. use multiple processes and diverse perspectives to explore alternative solutions

5. Digital Citizenship

Students understand human, cultural, and societal issues related to technology and practice legal and ethical behavior. Students:

    a. advocate and practice the safe, legal, and responsible use of information and technology

    b. exhibit a positive attitude toward using technology that supports collaboration, learning, and productivity

    c. demonstrate personal responsibility for lifelong learning

    d. exhibit leadership for digital citizenship

6. Technology Operations and Concepts

Students demonstrate a sound understanding of technology concepts, systems, and operations. Students:

    a. understand and use technology systems

    b. select and use applications effectively and productively

    c. troubleshoot systems and applications

    d. transfer current knowledge to the learning of new technologies

Other Standards Used Throughout the Units

American Association of School Librarians (AASL). (2007).
Standards for the 21st-Century Learner.
www.ala.org/ala/mgrps/divs/aasl/guidelinesandstandards/
learningstandards/standards.cfm

American Council on the Teaching of Foreign Language (ACTFL). (1996).
National Standards for Foreign Language Education.
www.actfl.org/i4a/pages/index.cfm?pageid=3392

International Reading Association and National Council of Teachers of English
(IRA/NCTE). (1996).
Standards for the English Language Arts.
www.reading.org/General/Publications/Books/bk889.aspx?mode=redirect

National Council for the Social Studies (NCSS). (2008).
NCSS Curriculum Standards for Social Studies Update-draft.
www.socialstudies.org/standards/taskforce/fall2008draft

Teachers of English to Speakers of Other Languages (TESOL). (1997).
ESL Standards for Pre-K–12 Students (online edition).
www.tesol.org/s_tesol/seccss.asp?CID=113&DID=1583

World-Class Instructional Design and Assessment (WIDA) Consortium. (2007).
English Language Proficiency (ELP) Standards Grades 6-12.
http://wida.wceruw.org/standards/elp.aspx

Unit
Worksheets

"I've Been Waiting For You" Radio Drama

Overview

You will enact the dialogue below as a given set of characters (spies, burglars, pet shop clerks, etc.) You must write and speak narration at the beginning and end of the dialogue, say the lines of dialogue as your characters, and add music and sound effects.

[Narrator describes the situation before the dialogue. Write this in 50 words or less.]

Person 1:	I've been waiting for you.
Person 2:	I'm sorry I'm late.
Person 1:	That's OK.
Person 2:	Thank you.
Person 1:	I have something for you.
Person 2:	What is it?
Person 1:	This.
	(**Note:** What is "This" and how will you convey it to your audience via audio?)

[Narrator describes what happens after the dialogue. Write this in 30 words or less.]

Think about what types of music and sound effects that you will use in this scene.

"I've Been Waiting For You" Radio Drama

Planning

You have to create and stay in character using voice inflections and tone. You also must write and read original narration to begin and end the scene. You cannot change the dialogue at all. You must also add one or two sound effects and music.

Beginning Narration (no more that 50 words)

_____

_____

Ending Narration (no more than 30 words)

_____

_____

What is "this" and how will you convey it to your audience? Narration, sound effects? Both?

_____

On the timeline below indicate what and where you will add music and sound effects.

| Beginning Narration | I've been waiting for you. | I'm sorry I'm late. | That's OK. |

——▶

| Thank you. | I have something for you. | What is it? | This. | Ending Narration |

——▶

Sound Effect/Music   Source (i.e., the Web address or "original")

_____   _____

Use the script below to cite the audio resources that you use.

> The music for this project came from the Creative Commons Mixter <<Say Original File Name(s)>> with a <<Say Type of License>>.

> The Sound Effects for this project came from the Free Sounds Project <<Say Original File Name(s)>>. All sound effects have a Creative Commons Sampling 1.0 Plus license.

Ungrateful Son Script

Roles: 12 narrators, husband, wife, neighbor, father

Narrator 1:   A husband and his wife were once sitting by the door of their house.

Narrator 2:   And they had a roasted chicken set before them and were about to eat it together.

Husband: Mmm. This chicken looks good.

Wife: Yes, it certainly does.

[Sound effect: whistling]

Husband: Here comes my father down the road. Look through the window and see him. Let's hide this chicken in the closet.

[Sound effects: footsteps and knocking at door]

Narrator 3:   The father came in and took a drink.

Father: Thanks for the water. See you soon.

Narrator 4:   The father left.

Narrator 5:   The son went to get the roasted chicken from the closet.

Narrator 6:   When he grabbed it, it turned into a giant frog…

Narrator 7:   …that jumped on the man's face.

[Sound effect: frog ribbit]

Husband: *[Angry]* What happened to my chicken? What is this frog doing on my face?

[Sound effect: frog ribbit]

Narrator 8:   The frog stayed on the man's face forever.

Narrator 9:   If any one wanted to take it off, it looked venomously at the person, as if it would jump on his or her face.

Narrator 10:	No one dared to touch it.
Narrator 11:	When the man walked down the street a neighbor said,
Neighbor:	Oh boy, that frog looks pretty mean. I don't want him on my face. Keep away from me!
Narrator 12:	And the ungrateful son was forced to feed the frog every day.

Audio Files

You must create and record three original sound effects yourself (person whistling, knocking at door, and footsteps).

The frog ribbit sound effect may be downloaded here (you will have to register for this site.):

> http://freesound.iua.upf.edu/samplesViewSingle.php?id=50406

Five music files may be downloaded here. They are each approximately 10–15 seconds long. You need to choose one:

> http://ccmixter.org/files/cs272/14300

Giving Credit

After the music at the end of your audio play, you need to read the following credits. You need to say:

> "The song *<<name of song>>* came from CCMixter.org.
> The frog sound effect, 50406_cs272_Frog_Ribbit.mp3, came from the
> Free Sounds Project."

This will allow a listener to find the music and sound effects afterwards and give the creator the credit he or she deserves.

The Metamorphosis: Audio Play Scripting

Script for Scene from *The Metamorphosis*

Characters: Gregor Samsa, Gregor's mother, Gregor's father, Gregor's sister, chief clerk

[The scene opens with music]

Narrator: As Gregor Samsa awoke one morning from uneasy dreams he found himself transformed into a gigantic insect. He was lying on his hard, as if it were armor plated, back, and when he lifted his head a little he could see his dome-like brown belly divided into stiff arched segments… his numerous legs, which were pitifully thin compared to the rest of his bulk, waved helplessly before his eyes.

Gregor: *[speaking in a squeaky bug voice]* What has happened to me?

[alarm clock rings]

Gregor's mother: Gregor, it's a quarter to seven. Hadn't you a train to catch?

Gregor: *[speaking in a squeaky bug voice]* Y-y-y-y-e-s-s-s. Thank you, Mother.

[loud knock at Gregor's door]

Gregor's father: Gregor? *[Knocking]* Gregor! What's the matter with you?

Gregor's sister: Gregor? Aren't you well? Are you needing anything?

Gregor: *[speaking in a squeaky bug voice]* I-l-l-l-m-m-m-m *[long pause)]* j-j-j-j-ust *[pause]* getting ready.

Gregor's sister: *[whispering]* Gregor, open the door, do.

Gregor: *[speaking to himself]* But what's the use of lying idle in bed. How did I get all of these legs? If I could just move this big belly of mine and get off the bed. *[loud thud]* Ouch!

[doorbell rings]

Gregor's sister: Gregor, the chief clerk's here.

Mr. Samsa:	Gregor, the chief clerk has come and wants to know why you didn't catch the early train. We don't know what to say to him. Besides, he wants to talk to you in person. So, open the door, please.
Chief clerk:	*[calling loudly]* Good morning, Mrs. Samsa.
Gregor's mother:	He's not well.
Gregor's father:	*[loudly]* He's not well, sir, believe me. What else would make him miss the train! The boy thinks about nothing but his work… he just sits there quietly at the table reading a newspaper or looking through railway timetables. The only amusement he gets is doing fretwork. For instance, he spends two or three evenings cutting out a little picture frame; you would be surprised to see how pretty it is…
Gregor:	*[in a squeaky bug voice, but slowly and carefully]* I'm just coming.
Gregor's father:	Well, can the chief clerk come in now?
Gregor:	No.
Chief clerk:	Mr. Samsa, what's the matter with you? Here you are, barricading yourself in your room, giving only "yes" and "no" for answers, causing your parents a lot of unnecessary trouble and neglecting—I mention this only in passing—neglecting your business duties in an incredible fashion…
Gregor:	But sir, I'm just going to open the door any minute. A slight illness, an attack of giddiness, has kept me from getting up… I can still catch the eight o'clock train.
Chief clerk:	Did you understand a word of it?
Gregor's mother:	Perhaps he's terribly ill and we're tormenting him… Did you hear how he was speaking?
Chief clerk:	That was no human voice… Just listen to that, he's turning the key.

[sound of lock and key turning]
[sound of door opening]

Chief clerk: Oh!

Gregor's mother: Ohhhh…

[sound of Gregor's mother passing out and falling to the floor]
[sound of Gregor's father crying]

Gregor: Well, I'll put on my clothes at once, pack up my samples and start off.

Gregor's mother: Help, for God's sake, help!

[sound of table being knocked over and coffee spilling onto the floor]

Gregor: Mother, mother.

[sound of Gregor's mother's scream]

Chief clerk: Ugh!

[sound of running down the steps and door slamming]

Gregor's father: Shoo, shoo! Get back!

[sound of feet stamping]
[sound of Gregor's father hissing]

Gregor's father: Get back in there!

[sound of door slamming]

Shakespearean Audio Drama

Act 3, Scene 3 of *Julius Caesar*

Read the following scene from Shakespeare's *Julius Caesar*. This is what you will be turning into an audio play. Although the only stage directions are the characters entering, there are many actions that can be inferred. Through the medium of audio you will convey these actions as well as the setting for the scene.

Caesar has just been assassinated and the Roman citizens are rioting. Cinna the poet, who has no other part in the play except for here, is wandering the dangerous streets of Rome.

[Scene]

Cinna the Poet:	Directly, I am going to Caesar's funeral.
First Citizen:	As a friend or an enemy?
Cinna the Poet	As a friend.
Second Citizen:	That matter is answered directly.
Fourth Citizen:	For your dwelling—briefly.
Cinna the Poet:	Briefly, I dwell by the Capitol.
Third Citizen:	Your name, sir, truly.
Cinna the Poet:	Truly, my name is Cinna.
First Citizen:	Tear him to pieces; he's a conspirator.
Cinna the Poet:	I am Cinna the poet, I am Cinna the poet.
Fourth Citizen:	Tear him for his bad verses, tear him for his bad verses.
Cinna the Poet:	I am not Cinna the conspirator.
Fourth Citizen:	It is no matter, his name's Cinna; pluck but his name out of his heart, and turn him going.
Third Citizen:	Tear him, tear him! Come, brands ho! fire-brands: to Brutus', to Cassius'; burn all: some to Decius' house, and some to Caasca's; some to Ligarius': away, go!

Shakespearean Audio Drama

Instructions

To produce the audio play you will need to do the following steps:

1. **Enact the parts.** Create unique voices for each of the five characters with speaking parts (Cinna, First Citizen, Second Citizen, Third Citizen, and Fourth Citizen). Speak all of the lines with credibility and emotion. The "voice" you use for each character should be consistent for that character throughout the scene.

   - How will you make each character sound unique?

   - How will you change their voices?

   - How will you remember what voice goes with what character?

   - How can the audio editing software help with this part?

2. **Add background music.** Add some background music and put it where it's appropriate (the whole scene does not need it).

   - Will it be fast or slow?

   - Will it be modern or classical?

   - Will the music stay the same or change over time?

   - When will the volume be low?

   - When will it be loud?

3. **Add sound effects.** Including "sounds" of citizens without speaking parts in the scene.

   - What kind of street is it? Noisy? Quiet? What kinds of sounds can give the feeling of quiet?

4. **Create a single file.** Create a single mp3 file with all of these elements.

Media Review

Content and Audience

1. Title of work being reviewed _____

2. Type of media (book, TV show, movie, etc.) _____

3. Audience for podcast (teens, adults, general) _____

4. What two or three facts about this topic can you reasonably assume your audience already knows and do not need to mention (e.g., Harry Potter is a character in a book, video games are popular with teenagers, *American Idol* is a TV show)?

5. What ideas about this topic might your audience not know or might they need to be reminded of (e.g., this is the latest Harry Potter book, *Guitar Hero 2* is an extremely popular video game, Paula Abdul is a judge on *American Idol*)?

Media Review

Media Review Template

The six items below should be the elements of your review. You can rearrange or modify these items. You should use these answers as the script for your audio recording.

1. Introduction (two or three sentences to interest the listener)

2. Factual description of specific media (objectively and briefly describe exactly what you are reviewing)

3. Context (how it relates to other episodes, games, books by the author, e.g., "This is the second version of the game.")

4. General opinion (one or two sentences). Your opinion does not have to be an absolute "I loved the movie because" or "I hated it because." It can be shaded, such as "It's not as good as the last, but… " or "I was expecting… and got… "

5. Specific points of interest, likes and/or dislikes with reasons and/or examples (expands on your general opinion)

6. Recommendation to listener (Yes/no? For all? For some? Who? Why?)

Citizen Journalists

Instructions

This week we are meeting for the first time. You all want to start putting your stories on the Internet—BUT WAIT!

- Before you can record your story, you have to write your story.

- Before you write your story, you have to find some news.

How do you go about writing a journalism story? Any ideas?

Below is a good website about being a reporter. Take a look:

www.courses.vcu.edu/ENG-jeh/BeginningReporting/Introduction/home.htm.

This website will be invaluable to you in learning reporting skills. The more you check this out, the more professional your reporting will be. I especially recommend the section on interviewing. If you are going to interview someone, remember:

a. You must have a script.

b. You must get their permission.

c. They must see the questions ahead of time (though their answers will be on air).

d. You must hear the interview before it is put on the Internet and approve (make a permission slip).

e. I will listen to any articles and interviews before they are put on the Internet.

You can also find books in the library about journalism.

EPR
ROOK FOR LOAN